AF344300

ONE IMMORTAL BEING

GRASSINI. One of the greatest opera singers in Italy.

MARIE LOUISE PETTYJOHN at age 24.

One Immortal Being

by

MARIE LOUISE PETTYJOHN

PHILOSOPHICAL LIBRARY
New York

Copyright © 1975, by Philosophical Library, Inc.
15 East 40 Street, New York, New York 10016

Library of Congress Catalog Card No. 75-7966
SBN 8022-2168-8

Manufactured in the United States of America

DEDICATION

This book has been written according to the dedication many years ago, to the service of God and my fellow man.

The challenge of this life has been the conquest of overcoming the material appearances of truth, and to fully know, and realize the infallible truth of the supremacy and reality of spirit.

Materialism binds the perceptions of spirit.

CONTENTS

INTRODUCTION

This book has been written to validate the strong evidence of the continuity of life. One lifetime being like one day at school. The law of cause and effect is always in operation.

Every immortal being has lived through several thousand incarnations. There is no end to evolvement.

This story is the full recall account of One Immortal Being, during only fourteen incarnations over a period of seventy thousand years.

Although there is nothing the soul does not know—the true data contained in this little book covers only a few of its experiences.

The data is true, or it would not have been written.

1

John, My Virgin Sweetheart

John was his name. He was very tall, big, blue-eyed, and beauty that would put a god to shame. But of this, he never seemed aware. He was very young but well educated. After college he had two years post graduate work at the University of Pennsylvania. His major was genetics. He also possessed a beautiful baritone voice. He was the only child of prominent parents, and sole heir to his grandparents' estate.

This is an ordinary introduction to a story that is not at all ordinary. Even our first meeting was extraordinary.

John had been on tour for several months with a production where I knew quite well a number of the members. I had been a voice student since fourteen years of age, and knew some months before, I was going to be a prima donna. Grand opera was my life, heart and soul.

John's company had just returned that evening from the tour. I had never heard anything about John. I lingered on to talk to some of my returning friends. I did not get back to where I had a room until about 9:00 p.m. I did not suspect a thing as I climbed the two flights to get to my room. I was amazed at what greeted me. The lights were on in my room, the door was wide open, the trunk had been pulled open. But the next room to mine held the tableau. My photographs were scattered all over the bed, and a strange, handsome man seemed to be in full charge. He had a look on his face that he had no intention of budging an inch. Jack, the boy whose room it was, looked like he'd had it. I asked him what was going on. He told me "this crazy galoot" came bounding up the steps two at a time and gasped "where's the girl?" Jack answered "what girl?" John said "Marie Louise, I was told she had a room here." Jack continued that he was practically forced to go to my room and get some photographs. Since Jack was pint-sized, he did have a point.

At about this time, John and I had the first good look at each other. I thought "you sure are wonderful and beautiful." I don't know what John thought. I only knew what he said: "I have been in love with you for months." I said "How could you when you have just now met me?" John then explained that for several months he had been on tour with people who knew me very well. They kept telling him I sure was the girl for him. "She is just like you, no hanky panky," all about the beautiful voice, etc. Anyway, they sure sold John a bill of goods.

At this point, I had no idea of what had become of Jack. We just stood there looking at each other. John said "I am sure now everything is perfect." But it was not destined to be so. It could have been, or might have been. For love exists because of that supreme original source. How much of radiance and joy depends on how much we love God and our fellow man.

Otherwise, poor blundering man must live with, and fight their personal demons. To name a few: hate, cruelty, injustice, greed, dishonesty and jealousy. John's demon was jealousy. It is high on the list because it is the destroyer of love.

To continue with our story—John's courtship was most enthusiastic and ardent. But I had a strange feeling it was a little peculiar. He wanted to be with me every waking minute. He lived on the second floor and would call up the stairs-well to find out if I were dressed. If the answer was yes, he would come the usual way—two steps at a time. We walked, talked and did business all over Chicago. At home he loved to romp and play. He could hardly keep his hands off me. But we were very happy, congenial and gay. Not the slightest friction or disagreement. We sang a lot together. Our favorite was "Sweethearts" from Maytime. We made the most thrilling and heavenly song together. "Ah, love is so sweet in the springtime, when blossoms are fragrant in May. No years that are coming can bring time to make me forget, dear, this day. I'll love you in life's grey December, the same as I love you today."

But John never took me in his arms and kissed me.

Our first application to work as a double resulted in two single engagements. I was the first. Then I went home for a visit. The plans were for John to come to meet my parents as soon as his engagement was over.

For some days I never heard a word from John. I was deeply disturbed. But never in my life I lifted a finger to hold a man my love could not hold.

Finally a letter did come telling about a big worry he had. But it had been resolved and there was no need for further worry. But he could not tell me about it and asked me please not to ask. John had returned to Chicago for a while. He followed the letter very quickly and came for the promised visit to my home.

The first moment we were alone he opened those big arms and held me tightly. Believe it or not, he gave me a kiss that felt like all heaven had turned loose. When I could come up for air, I said "John, I thought you would never get around to this." His answer stupified me. "You are just too impatient." For once I was speechless.

A few days after John's visit, I returned to Chicago. A day or so later John's landlady called up and said, "Come down, I have something funny to tell you." After she started talking and laughing, I was so distressed I heard only parts of her funny story about when John was on his singing engagement, a woman in the next hotel room started to cough. Then John coughed, and this kept up for some time until John went to her room where she seduced him. That put him in a frenzy of fear that he had picked up a disease. He had to have several doctors' opinions that all was well. I begged the lady not to tell John that she had told me. She promised, and I feel sure he never found out that I knew.

My beautiful love who had denied me his kisses was seduced by some hussy whose name he probably never knew. I picked up the pieces and went on loving him.

A few days more went happily by. Then we opened in Milwaukee for several weeks of light opera.

This is where I must bring Al into the picture if we are to continue our story. Al lived in Milwaukee, a second-generation German. About a year previously, we had been engaged. We thought we were very much in love. But looking back, I think it was mostly propinquity. I had known him for several weeks, but paid no attention to him or any other man in the company. We travelled on trains, and Al asked if he could sit by me. This continued until we always sat together while traveling. I enjoyed talking and visiting with him.

I shall never forget his first kiss, because it was my first kiss. As usual, it was most unusual. I was looking over the bulletin board. Al came along just then and we were alone for the moment. He gave me what I would describe as a very tender love kiss. I tried to act as if it were routine. I was very nonchalant. But I didn't get away with it. A few minutes later in my dressing room, I fainted dead away. When discovered, most thought I was acting funny by putting heavy white mask all over my face and purple eye shadow on my lips. While I was still a little sick and groggy, a certain lovable but devilish Jim bent over me and said, "Maybe in the future you will be more careful how you hand out your favors."

I knew after a time that it would be difficult for us to build a happy life together, because he had the German idea that men were superior to women in every way. The man should run the show of marriage in full control. That didn't appeal to me one little bit. We disagreed and sometimes even quarreled. It was the old Adam story that God created women as an after-thought, so that men would not get lonely. Even so, we thought we loved each other. Al got ambitious and decided to become a chiropractic doctor. He asked me to wait two years for him. That seemed like such a long time to wait. But I consented, and went to New York where I signed a contract. I didn't know at the time that I was replacing another leading lady. I was not popular because they all wanted the other girl back. She wanted back and I wanted out. The manager tried to arrange things and sent a wire to the show owner in New York. The reply came back to "make any changes you wish but retain Miss Pettyjohn." Just before this Al made a trip to see me and asked me to marry him at once. I refused because I had signed a contract. But his idea was for me to just jump the show. I flatly refused for I would never do such a thing. Al had given up all idea of becoming a doctor. So that proud German broke down and sobbed that he could not live without me.

I was not happy in this production. I wrote Al a blue letter and complained we would not be in this mess if he had carried out his plans to become a doctor. Al answered with a rude letter. He wrote, "the next time you feel a fit coming on, just stick your head in a bucket of cold water." I very gently broke our engagement.

Now back to our opening in Milwaukee; I had ceased to love Al for some time. But I had an idea that I would like to see him once more for a few minutes. I wanted a final settlement of my mind. To know it was all finished or the end of a cycle.

For in true love as God intended it to be, it is not all physical. A large part lives in the heart and soul. Just as the soul survives physical death and lives forever. So does anything that has ever been a part of the soul, also survives a little.

I explained a little of this to John and asked if it would cause him any pain, or doubt, if I saw Al for a few minutes. He heartily agreed and thought it a good idea. He joked with others about it and said, "I am turning over my girl to another man, for just a few minutes, but right now she is mine." I should have been warned by that remark, but then I thought all was sunshine and happiness. How wrong I was, for when I returned, not more than twenty minutes later, John was gone. The mission was easy and successful; I was eager to be with my love again.

I could not find John anywhere. He told me later that he had taken in the late shows and then walked the streets until nearly dawn. John looked so haggard and unhappy. I weep even now as I relive it in order to write it just as it was lived. He said, very defiantly, "your grandchildren can tell about how you nearly drove their grandfather crazy."

I tried so hard to reassure him and love the hurt away. But he decided to forego the grandfather bit and have nothing more to do with me. I was deeply distressed, but my pride would not let him see me unhappy. So I always put on a show of life and gayety, but I sure didn't want any part of any man. For the moment, I had a bad case of indigestion where men were concerned.

As the show broke up after the last performance, I cornered John. It wasn't easy; he wouldn't even look at me. But I stood firm and asked him, since we would never see each other again, couldn't we part as friends with good wishes for the future? He just turned and walked away. Love dies very hard for me.

But we were destined to meet again under the strangest and almost unbelievable circumstances .

A few minutes later, while I still had on what I thought was a glamorous make-up and costume, I was contacted by a man from the Marx Brothers who were also playing in Milwaukee. He told me they needed a singer with a beautiful big voice to play the role of Grouchos, a forty-five year old wife who hen-pecked her husband. Then he added, "I think you suit the part to perfection." I said, "no thank you, I am not interested." But he finally persuaded me to meet the Marx Brothers the next morning. I was not at all interested until Groucho started to talk. He said, "The irony of show business, you try so hard to find someone with youth and beauty, but what do you get—too much age and not enough beauty." "But just this once, the requirements do not call for youth and beauth, but what do we get? You guessed it, we get youth and beauty." "She is much too young for the part." But the man who had contacted me took over and said, "what are we, hams or artists? Besides, you haven't heard her sing and that is the main requirement."

So we proceeded to the green room where I met Chicko and Harpo. They were magnificent musicians on the piano and harp. When we three got started we couldn't stop; it was one number after another. It was joyous. But finally they broke us up to talk business. By then it was a strong three vote for yes and a very weak no vote.

I came back the next day with an evening gown. They all went to work on my face. When they had finished all the damage they could do, I looked like someone's great grand-mother. But the resemblance to Dracula was remarkable.

I signed the contract with the mental reservation that no one but me would ever put on the make-up and I would not look a day over forty-five. After all, it was to be a vacation trip of six weeks, two in London, Paris and Berlin. But before rehearsal time the foreign money markets had dropped so low that the trip was canceled. I was more relieved than disappointed.

Next, I went back to New York where I was putting together a twenty minute version of the opera Pagliacci. In seeking operatic talent, I met Charles Trier who was rated as the world's greatest operatic coach. His was the final word if it ever came to a difference of opinion on the dramatic action of the opera. I became almost at once his scholarship pupil. He was seventy-two and retired but no one was going to stop that old war horse. He rented a large rehearsal hall in the heart of the theatrical district, a good pianist and a lot of chairs. Then he began coaching talented artists of his own choosing. He was small and wiry and could jump through the air quicker and lighter than any cat I ever saw. He was half French and the only living person who could teach the French system of body technique. It was very difficult to learn or teach but with the right material and abilities, those who mastered it became superb artists of the dramatic action of the opera ."Daddy Trier," as we called him, used to tell about how little the Italians knew about any kind of dramatic action. He said they simply held out one arm for five or ten minutes, and then the other arm, as if to hold up traffic. He said there were two American opera singers who knew just a little of the French technique.

Now more about Charles Trier. I was amazed as I watched him work. I never dreamed a coach could be so brilliant, powerful and magnetic. Every fibre of my being became super-charged. Trier came over to me and said, "I believe I could make a red-blooded actress out of you." "You," I answered, "could make a red-blooded actress out of a piece of stone." We started to work the next morning.

I was enthusiastic and started to turn on my stuff. He simply tore me to pieces. I didn't mind that part, but I felt heartsick that he would not continue to work with me. I would take anything if he would only continue to coach me. Later he called out to me, "let's try it again." I jumped up happily and said, "you are still going to work with me?" He threw back his head and said, "I hope you don't think I give up that easily."

The very hard work continued for several weeks; I was black and blue over parts of my body from learning the French way to die and other difficult scenes.

As time went on, we progressed and "Daddy Trier" became very gentle. He softly whispered instructions directly into my ear, first from one side and then the other as the action required. This is where his cat talents came in. No matter how fast I went up or down stage, he was always there ahead of me with his soft whisperings. It had to be this way because I was singing the heavy dramatic role of Nedda. Others in the cast had been so well trained by Trier, he could put all his attention on me.

I noticed the audiences were getting larger all the time. Trier said people were getting curious about me and were asking questions like "just who is she?" Some said I was the greatest opera singer they had ever heard. Trier said that he acted mysterious and said, "we have very big people in this studio."

Trier knew exactly who I was because he was an occultist, as are most artists. I had told him I was directly descended from a favorite singer at the Court of Napoleon. She was a French woman. Trier then asked me what her name was and I told him it was Annie Grace. He corrected me and said, "her name was Annie Gracé, pronounced Grosay. She was Irish but married a Frenchman. She was the greatest grand opera singer in the world at her time."

I am happy to record now a moment of great adulation. We had just finished the twenty-minute version, without any coaching. Mr. Trier took me by the hand and drew me nearer to him and made a speech as follows: "When this girl first started, she was a little discouraged. But she has accomplished in six weeks what I thought was not humanly possible to accomplish in less than six months." He continued, "I have known the work of every prominent Nedda since the opera was first produced. About 50 percent of them, I have personally trained. But I can stand here now and tell you that there has never been a greater performance of Nedda than the one you saw and heard tonight."

Annie Grace will appear again before this book is finished, but her introduction at this time is necessary.

A singer has a more complicated problem than any other type of artist. The body is all important, because it contains all the tools and implements of singing. Certain physical formations are necessary. A high bridged nose, wide throat, very high dome in the roof of the mouth and a flat back-of-the-head are required. Besides all this and much more, there must be the phenomenal vocal chords. An opera singer is no accident. So, at times, it becomes necessary to sort of mend the fences, such as having children in order to reincarnate again in a hundred or more years in their own blood lines, so as to be able to pick up their own precious genes. An opera singer is for all eternity.

But, since this part of the story is mostly my love life and not my career, let's go back and finish off John.

It was December and quite dark except for the bright neon signs at about 5:30 P.M. I was sitting alone in a closed and deserted office where I had finished my business a little earlier. The outer office was always unlocked. I was resting and waiting for the next appointment, when I heard someone clattering down the steps from the third floor. The elevators were all running. The steps stopped just outside the door where I was sitting. I became a little uneasy and when the door opened, I was frozen with fear. But not for long; John entered the half dark room and was just as surprised as I. He said that when he got to that door, he seemed to get the impression that if he opened the door, he would find me. He was excited and happy and full of regrets that he had lost me, and had constantly prayed that he would find me again. I began to get practical and told him that I would not marry any man in show business. I had seen too many sad and unhappy situations when theatrical people had to put their children in a boarding school after they reached school age. I vowed that would never happen to me. John said quickly that he would get out of show business at once. He even promised to go out tomorrow and buy me any kind of home anywhere I wanted it.

His father was delighted when he called him that night and said he wanted to get out of show business and get married. He also said he wanted to get into banking. His father said that he would start pulling strings at once.

The burnt child dreads the fire, so I started pouring on cold water. I told him about Jack who was thirty years or more older than I. I was not in love with him, but he was a constructive friend, and the first one to teach me how to think for myself and not to place limitations on my abilities. He seemed to think I could do anything. He was the highest paid writer in show business and one of the greatest extemporaneous speakers. He sold more liberty bonds during the first World War than any other individual. He was also a musician and played most instruments except the piano. The violin was his favorite. Jack was full-blooded Irish for countless generations.

I told John I had no idea of suddenly kicking Jack overboard just because he had suddenly reappeared. He was indignant that I could have such a thought about him. "I would never kick the stool out from under an old man."

I confess I had very negative thoughts about John and I ever getting together again although I still loved him very much. I agreed to talk to Jack right away and tell him that John had returned. But before I could tell Jack anything, he told me he had seen me walking down Broadway with my John. He went on about how proud he was of us—that never had a more beautiful couple walked on Broadway. He then added, "now that's the man you should marry."

But when I returned to the little apartment I shared with a cute little gal who was a dress designer, John had called and found me out. He knew I was talking to Jack as planned. He took off like a kite and left word he had signed up with a company leaving at once. I was crushed again, but not as bad as the first time. This time it was for life and maybe forever.

I am sorry this story does not have a happy ending like stories should have. This is a true story; nothing has been changed. So, we must take the facts and find a happy ending. I did not grieve too much because I knew I had been saved from an unhappy marriage. But I did grieve that John had so little chance of finding happiness in marriage.

Life belongs to the strong. One must win the gift of happiness by meeting and overcoming little demons. John promised so much but delivered so little.

With Al it was different. I could have easily handled his little aberrations about the male superiority. What really broke our engagement was that he did not measure up to the high standards I had for my mate. For after making definite plans to become a doctor, he gave up so easily. I do not admire quitters.

My blessings go out to the wonderful men who have loved me and enriched my life.

2

Bill, The Unpredictable Millionaire

Bill was quite a man, brilliant in repartee, wit and humor, with a deep sense of responsibility. Above all things, he was an ardent seeker after truth, with a curious probing mind that could only lead him to occult study and research.

As time went on, he felt that his absorbing interest in things not obvious was taking abilities away from business which he also loved and desired. He was the sole owner of a large and successful business. He finally decided to put his business affairs first and occult study second, like a delightful dessert enjoyed after a hearty meal. I believe the strong sixth sense he developed through occult study contributed greatly to his wealth. It is necessary to have a healthy balance in all things, especially so in occult study.

I was not aware of Bill's fine character, mental and spiritual attainments when I first met him, under the most strained and adverse circumstances. I thought I had reason to believe he was a big, bad wolf interested only in conquest.

At this time, I was working from a real estate firm and had been given a ride to the city to do some shopping. I was to meet the boss before 5:00 P.M. for the ride back home. He was making a big real estate deal with Bill. When I returned to the car, the boss was all excited about the real estate deal, plus a little side deal he made to bring me to meet Bill. He would wait for us at his office. I flatly refused and told the boss he had a license to peddle real estate but that didn't include me. The boss became uneasy and upset, as he only had a binder on the deal, and was afraid he might lose both the deal and the rich client if he failed to take me to his office. I tried to be reasonable and asked what possible interest his client could have in me. He said he told him I was one of the prettiest girls in the state. That did it! Using me for bait! I retorted, "you prove my point." "Oh, no," he said, "I fully explained what a nice girl you are and he said 'that is just the kind of girl I would like to meet.'" We fussed and fumed about it until I realized there was a way to handle the situation that would be satisfactory to me and get the boss off the hook, and would hurt no one. So, I consented to meet his client, but made up my mind that I would be nothing but icy politeness. We drove to the office and six feet, 225 pounds of sheer wolf (I thought) came to the car for the introduction.

The wolf invited me to have dinner with him and said that he would drive me home. I held my head very high and in a cold dignified manner thanked him politely and refused, saying that my family was expecting me home. I felt proud that I was carrying it off so well as planned. Suddenly the unexpected happened. The wolf did not like the way things were going and took over instantly by reaching into the car and pulling the rather large hat down over my face and then roaring with laughter that made a shambles of me, because I couldn't stop laughing either. I lost track of the boss about that time. All tension and dignity were gone, which left the wolf in full charge. Anyway, I didn't go to dinner with him.

A few days later he loomed up big and bold at the door of my home, happy and all smiles. We went for a little drive and parked by a lake. He tried to kiss me but I fought him off. This brought up a disagreement over a year later. He said he wrote in his diary that at the lake-side was the first time he kissed me. I denied the kiss and asked him if he considered that little something that brushed against my cheek, a kiss?

Bill didn't return again to my home for a year, but he did write a letter asking for my friendship and saying that he could promise he would never do anything to make me regret it. He asked me to telephone my answer. I chose not to answer because I still thought he was probably a wolf. What a doubting Thomas I have always been. There is still time to correct that.

A year went by before I saw him again. The friendship was resumed by sudden unexpected circumstances. I was visiting long time friends in the city when Bill's name was mentioned about being a high ranking mason, as was my host. I casually mentioned that I knew him, that he had wanted to date me and that I refused because, being a rich man, I thought he was just out to make me. My host was horrified that I could be so misled. He told me Bill was highly responsible and a high grade man. He knew Bill quite well. He said there was not a woman in the city who would not be delighted to receive his attentions. My girl friend thought I was lying about knowing Bill and refusing to date him. I was shocked and asked, "you mean you don't believe me?" She just gave me a silly sly grin and said nothing. I was slightly infuriated and said, "just sit still a few minutes until I can get to the telephone and I will prove it." So, I called Bill and, in a sweet casual tone which implied I had seen him during the last few days, asked if he had anything on for tonight. His surprised voice said, "no, where are you, hold the phone a minute until I can write down the address." After he went for the pen I could hear him singing at the top of his voice. He said, "I will call for you at 5:30. I have waited a year for this call." I gazed at my friend with a withering look and asked if she believed me now. My friend had nothing to say.

Bill and I had a very good dinner and a pleasant evening. He didn't try to kiss me. The next morning he called and asked if I would go with him to a nearby town where he had some business. I accepted but asked if I could bring my friend's small son, which was agreeable. On the date the evening before, I sat as far away from him as possible. I was still being careful. He sure got through to me that morning; the little boy was on the seat between us. Bill remarked that he couldn't stand a girl who sat in the car with him as far away as possible. He added, "Of course, this is different, we have the boy along and the seat is not too wide." After that, I sat reasonably close to him. After a few dates, I began to relax and settle down for a safe reserved friendship with a man twenty years older than I was. By this time, I had begun to have a little idea of his brilliant mind, the flashes of wit and humor, and his deep occult understanding.

On one date I have in mind, he walked toward the front door. I decided to go out and meet him to avoid the greetings, and as we were about to meet I gave him a smile. That was the last thing I remember clearly, for as sudden as lightning I was picked up and pitched way up in the air, with nothing but the thin air to hold me. As I came down, he caught me with a roar of laughter. All this in broad daylight in full view of friends and neighbors! I was so stunned, I couldn't pinpoint my feelings. One sure thing: friendship with Bill was not going to be dull.

During the next few weeks, he spent every week-end at my home. He felt so strange visiting in a private home. When he visited friends, he always went to a hotel. He enjoyed my family and we all had a pleasant time. Bill brought sensible and useful gifts such as a bottle of imported champagne and once a stalk of red bananas—the most delicious I ever tasted.

Somehow I don't remember the first kiss, but there must have been a first because we got into high gear very quickly.

Bill was enthusiastic and happy and I lost all awareness that he was twenty years older.

This happy state of affairs did not last very long. Bill had to get serious and asked me a loaded question. He said for me to take my time, he didn't expect an answer right away, but to give it careful consideration before answering. As I usually reach decisions quickly, I wondered why all the pussy-footing. Finally, he came up with his question, which was very simple, I thought. "If you were married, would your happiness depend on having children?" I laughed and told him I didn't need more than one second to answer that one, as I had given up a very promising operatic career which I loved with my heart and soul because I wanted children even more. How foolish can a person get? Nature plays some dirty tricks on us. I feel now that having children is one of the poorest games we can play. Bill sagged and slumped deeply. This I could not understand because I thought he was a man who would dearly love a family.

He told me a little later there was so little to do in my home town, he would discontinue his visits. But he insisted that whenever I was in the city, he wanted me to promise I would always call him. He wanted to keep in touch. I really didn't want to give Bill up either. So I did call him occasion- ally to sort of feel his pulse. It seemed strange to me that he never had an engagement when I called. I knew he was active socially and belonged to a number of clubs. He told me years later that he always had engagements every evening but he made an iron-bound rule that whenever Marie called, all other dates were off. At the same time, he told me I had given him the greatest love experience he had ever known. This was just a few weeks before he died.

Some time later, I had a glimmer of understanding when Bill came up with another far-out, strange topic for my opinion. He said the case he had in mind was strictly hypothetical: In a case that two people were married and wanted children and the wife could have children but the husband could not. He went on to gently explain how this situation could be overcome. There had to be a biological father who would be selected as to high intelligence, health, blood and character along with other desirable qualities. At this point, my thoughts raced out of control. I thought he sure is important; if such a man could be found why not have him for the father all the way? But I pushed such wild thoughts away. This concept did not go along with Bill's ideas. So I quieted down and listened to what he had to say. He continued, "The acting father would assume full responsibility and love such a child as his own, but the greater happiness would come knowing his wife would not be denied a child of her own. Didn't I think this would be vastly wiser than the couple who wait a long time to get just any child of questionable percentage?"

From a purely analytical viewpoint, I know now that Bill was right, but emotion has to be considered too, which is the great powerhouse of the universe. It is the very same power God uses in all His creations. Emotion is raw power; it does not think or compute. That is why we are given the analytical mind to act as a guide in handling the great power of emotion. I knew I was not ready to handle such power as Bill seemed so able to do.

So, as deeply devoted as I was to Bill, I had to hurt him again. I knew who were the hypothetical; and I confronted it fairly and squarely. I told him I would rather not have a child than to go the artificial route and wonder how a mother would feel when she looked at the baby she adored and knew it was not conceived in love. Bill was quiet for a time, but he did not slump.

This is not the end for Bill and me. He did not give up

easily. But I was seeking my true love and I don't give up easily either.

The months flew by and I stopped seeing Bill because a new romance had blossomed. Jack breezed in with so much charm and the knack of doing so many delightful things at the right time, such as unexpected gifts which were so appropriate: a special messenger to my home with flowers and a love letter. I was progressing too; Jack was only fifteen years older than I.

A high spot was an all day trip with another couple to attend the horse races in the city. Jack asked me to pick the horses I thought would win and he would place the bets. It was a big thrill as we never lost a bet. He told me about getting a tip on a horse named "Torture" to win the derby race. But to use my judgment as he didn't know whether the tip was good or not. At first I played hunches but soon had to get down to pure horse flesh. So a big part of the afternoon was spent back where the horses were walked around before every race. I studied them carefully, noticing the tiniest detail. I picked two horses I thought were the best for the big race: "Torture" and another beauty named "Firefly." I switched back and forth but finally settled on "Torture" to win the big race. Just as the horses started to run, I got my last hunch—too late to change it! It flashed into my mind that just as sure as "Torture" won, our romance would not have a happy ending, and it would be "torture" for both of us. My heart sank way down as "Torture" won, and "Firefly" came in a close second. Would to God it could have been the other way, with "Firefly" winning. But only God can tell when the tapestry of life is being woven what is best for all concerned.

I did not tell Jack about my foreboding; he was so very happy with life at the moment.

After the races, the four of us had a fine dinner and attended a top rated musical road show. After that, we had another late dinner at a famous restaurant. Then there was the pleasant relaxing drive home. It had been a big and exciting day. Jack was the personification of "Prince Charming."

That day life seemed enchanted. It was a vision of the joy and radiance life could hold. But my heart was heavy. Life did continue along story book happiness for a number of weeks more.

Then came dark despair, shock and confusion. Jack had a split personality. I don't know how he managed to hold on to the positive side for so long. But he had love and love is the greatest miracle worker. In fact, love is the cohesive force that holds the universe together. I was heart-broken, but the greatest sorrow was for Jack; his condition tore my heart to pieces. He seemed so helpless to fight the black moods which made him sullen, morose, depressed, withdrawn and highly critical. A black cloud or evil spirit seemed to hover over him. It was a complete collapse of his wonderful personality.

At that time, I knew so little about mental illness. Since then I have become very interested and concerned and gathered much data, but not nearly enough. I believe most illness can be cured if we could just find the cure. Mental illness is the most difficult of all to cure, because it is a sick-ness of the soul, not the body. That part of the being that never sleeps or dies. The mentally ill person somewhere along the time track took a wrong turn. There are so many wrong turns along the track. The classic example is selling one's soul to the devil or negation for material gain or non-existent pleasure not found on those wrong turns. Even a much more severe wrong turn is the cruelly crippling of body, mind or soul of a less powerful being. The doctors do not have the cure for severe illness of this kind. But it is the number one enemy the world faces today. If this situation cannot be handled we will not have a world fit for habitation. The problem is so great, we can only do our small part and send out thoughts of compassion, love and harmony. This is God's universe. He created it; we can only have faith in God's ability to handle His own affairs. When man utterly fails, God will take over to handle the problems too great for human solution.

I recall a moment of intense pain during one of the black moods when Jack looked at me with such a pleading and pitiful look and said, "During my good times, I try so hard to build up enough love to carry me through the bad times." At this moment his love, which is spiritual in nature, completely transcended the black mood.

I stood by for over a year and did everything I could. But all thought of marriage was out. There were a number of changes but Jack's love never changed. He took a position in another state. A few months later the sad news reached me that Jack was found dead in his hotel room. It was not discovered for two days. The new maids coming on duty thought he was a sleeping guest. It was not thought to have been suicide.

I suffered sharp grief and regret. But there was comfort to know the hard travail of this life was over for my beloved Jack.

I don't think the average person has very much understanding of the beauty and power of love which is a union of the physical and spiritual. It is as limitless as the stars in the firmament. The only limitation being the individual's capacity to love. Each one can and usually partakes of love to their full capacity. But the capacity varies from so little to so great. But whatever the capacity small or large it can be full to the brim. True love never dies; it will always be self-renewing and live forever. As I have experienced, there can be any number of loves, each a little different, but all in full measure to capacity.

Grim circumstances of life may take away the physical aspects, but love is always there to renew; with even a little understanding of love there can be no jealousy, which is negative, the very opposite of love.

When a being passes physical life and enters the great unobstructed universe, they find their loves, but with no sense of possession, only love. Then one can know this is a pretty good heaven. Realization will then dawn that life is a repeat performance. We live so many incarnations with a very few beings. Love is truly forever.

There are many mis-matings on this material plane, due to the frailty of this Earth, such as lack of vision beyond the five senses, the impatience of waiting for the right mate, which causes much compromise with marriage—or, marriage when used for material gain. Then love can and usually does die, which leaves a wreckage of broken hopes, misery and frustration. When love is dead, the marriage is dead and should be dissolved. There can be numbers of reasons why marriage is not advisable but there is only one valid reason for marriage and that is a deep love between two people. Then all other obstacles can be easily overcome.

Happily, I do not believe in the law of Karma as it is usually taught in the older occult schools. Karma is no more than the soul's own guilt complex, which is lightly laid in by the soul itself. It is not immutable in any sense of the word. After giving up the physical body, the soul goes through a period to take a good look at the life it has just lived. At this time the soul is very severe on itself, highly critical about the mistakes and wrong doing. After this, the postulates are made about what the next life will be. If the soul wishes to progress and improve the next life, the soul has the power to install limitations and circumstances to make sure the lesson will be learned. Of course, this is a little game souls play when not yet highly evolved. The quicker, surer way for the soul to use its vast powers, the soul need only take a look and then postulate how it desires it to be next time. The only variation to this is when the soul deliberately chooses evil when it knows better; that is when psychosis, light or severe, is laid in.

In a later chapter, we will deal entirely with the powers of the soul.

Just to make an educated guess in Jack's case would indicate he probably, at some time, chose evil over good, and injured others. In general, as in most things, the scale is gradient. Knowing Jack as I did, I think he played with evil lightly, just the outer rims, but knowingly. I believe he learned some lessons very well during his current life. Since I suffered over the situation, indications are that I played some part in a former life; probably I failed to guide and help him when I could have.

We are to some degree responsible for the people who come into our lives.

Since Bill is still playing a part in my life, now is the time to relate a strange communication from him.

On a trip to visit relatives, the bus stopped over for about twenty minutes where Bill lived. I did not get off the bus, but I head a voice tell me to get a paper. I answered mentally that I had a paper and didn't need another one. But the voice kept telling me to hurry and get a paper. I still refused; I wasn't about to let some voice from beyond make me do something silly. Then the voice became irritated and said, "Don't be so damn stubborn, if you get the paper you will see some big news on the front page." That got me. I hurriedly got off and bought a paper. But for some strange reason, I did not return to my seat; instead I took the small seat up front by the driver. I started to read the upper half of the front page. After looking at Hitler's picture, ranting and raving about all the violent things he was going to do. Thus the peculiar incident was forgotten. I became relaxed; some fifteen minutes later I turned the paper over to look at the bottom half. Instantly was the news in large type that Bill had died suddenly during the early morning hours; too short a time to write a full account. The shock was heavy and I resented Bill having to divide the front page with Hitler. All relaxation was gone; the tears could not be controlled. I realized some power had directed me to the little seat up front. Bill then, in his familiar natural voice, started to talk up a storm. He laughed so heartily as always, telling me funny stories in a happy carefree manner.

Then a few nights later during sleep, he brought the condition which had caused his death to my body, telling me about it and I feeling the big ball of gas he could not handle. Just as it reached his heart, he cried out in agony, "Oh Marie, I can't come out of this."

I had little hunches about when to see Bill for short visits. He also visited us at intervals. This with my blessed husband's full consent. The last visit was a few weeks before he died. He told me then I had given him the greatest love experience he had ever had. I never ceased to love Bill spiritually and I never will. I know any time I need him, he will always be on call. That is the wonderful thing about love.

3

An Interlude Before I Met My Husband

Time, as always, keeps rolling along. Now is the time to relate a lively little interlude which was a prologue to meeting Turnley, my husband.

I met an intriguing woman who lived next door to friends. We were attracted at once, and no wonder, for she was psychic, an artist in oils, had an engaging personality and a handsome young husband. But she looked somewhat like an old witch. The thought just occurs to me at this moment that she probably was accused of being a witch and got into serious trouble. After knowing her better, she seemed quite beautiful to me.

This brings up more data on the subject of witches. I had a friend who was a superlative artist on the piano. Once, when we were giving a concert together at a large auditorium, a few hours before curtain time my friend suffered acute stage fright. She remarked that she felt like she was about to be executed. That started me doing some soul searching but I never got the answer until several years later when she suffered a nervous breakdown. As soon as we could get together again, we walked up and down the street. It was the only way we could be alone. Her poor husband thought he had to protect her by keeping her under wraps. He was probably in the house biting his fingernails. During the walk, she told me a lot about her mental illness. The big light dawned with full understanding when she related how she had shrieked and screamed when she was led into a room with an open fireplace burning brightly. I knew then, beyond the slightest doubt, that she had been burned at the stake for a witch. She was so sensitive and aware, as artists are. For an unknown reason, nature had not turned off the valve of memory to protect the present life. It has been established that full recall is full sanity. But my precious friend did not have full recall, only a glimmer of awareness—enough to terrify and confuse, rather than clear. So many of the most gifted and valuable beings, including Joan of Arc, have suffered great physical, mental and spiritual shock over this.

Today we have progressed a long way from burning sensitive, gifted people. But in terms of civilization, we are still stuck in the mud. The problems we do not solve just grow bigger.

The biggest, most basic problem facing humanity today is how to handle the criminally insane. There is so little understanding of the magnitude of the problem and much less understanding in the solutions. This, I believe, is the biggest stumbling block in the path of man's struggle toward civilization. We should know the fact that any being who is destructively insane is in that condition through his own choosing. He deliberately, knowingly, along the path, took a very bad wrong turn and chose evil instead of good. There is nobody to blame but that individual himself. Therefore, an evil being cannot be allowed to wreck and kill as he desires. This brings up the next problem: what to do with such an offender.

In the low state of our civilization, we think we are doing fine when life imprisonment is decreed. This is a horrible, wrong thing to do to any being, no matter how evil. It is destructive to the entire society. The death penalty is far better for all concerned. This brings a little progress, but not nearly enough. The next step upward would be a humane death, a highly protective legal action, but no public execution, no walking the last mile, no hoards of eager beaver reporters dishing out the distressing details. All of our society is damaged by this. How much better for everyone to use just a little pill, gentle and painless, not even an emotional upset because the evil one need not know the purpose or when of the pill. There will not be a physical awakening. The being is then free to take another look, another choice. He will be helped all along the way, if he so desires.

In a civilized society, there is no blame, no sense of punishment or debt to society. Only what help can be given to the one who took a bad, destructive wrong turn.

There is a much higher, more glorious solution, but this cannot be taken until we can establish a much higher social order. This represents the rewards of evolvement. This solution is given directly from God. "There is a law irrevocably decreed in heaven before the foundation of the world, upon which all blessings are predicated." The law is: "All things must produce after their own kind." This law works from top to bottom, from the seed planting of all kinds through the animal and human to the highest spiritual levels. "Like shall attract like." So, if the majority of people in any society are not violent in thought or action, if their dominant thoughts are love of God and their fellow man, then they are safe as individuals of the society. Few evil beings can find birth on such a planet. This law is immutable and always works. Therefore, each civilization is fully responsible for what it attracts.

Now is a good time to leave the problems of witches and evil psychotics and go to flowers to bring this story back to the present time.

I had a beautiful garden of mixed flowers in full bloom. So I took two large bouquets on my next visit, one to the friends and one to the neighbor. The former witch gazed at the bouquet for a time and then said she was going to paint the flowers in oils and name it for me.

On a later visit, she called me over to see the finished picture. I was amazed at how beautiful it was—an exact duplicate, physically, of the bouquet. But how much more she had painted into it! She gave it eternal life and vitality, with an exquisite aura of ethereal beauty. I have always wondered how an artist with only a brush and paints can capture so much spiritual loveliness, but that is the special way with artists.

One glance told me the artist would never part with that creation. It may have been her masterpiece. I just took a long look, enough to hold some of the vision always.

There were plenty of lively aspects to her personality. She knew my friend Bill, and knew about the twenty years difference in our ages, and that I still carried the torch for him. She undertook my re-education in no uncertain terms. She wanted to know what in the world I wanted with a man twenty years older than I. She continued, "You have seen that handsome young man I am married to? Well, if anything should happen to him, God forbid, I would grab me off a much younger man."

During the next phase of the friendship, she read the cards for me. Of course, people who successfully read cards, coffee grounds, tea leaves or what have you, are just naturally psychic or telepathic. They just think there must be some physical contact. I have discovered in later years that the mind, or spirit, is fully sufficient for any contact anywhere.

After laying out the cards, the witch told me I was going to be married soon. As usual, I doubted. She insisted it was sure because I had drawn to me the strongest possible card combination for marriage. She then told me about an old maid friend. She had tried for years to get the right cards to bring marriage but she was never able to succeed in this.

She advised me to make my plans and to get the trousseau ready. Because there was no doubt. Less than a year later when the wedding day did come, the depression was in full force and the thought of a trousseau seemed far-fetched. I was so happy when I bought two new dresses, hat, shoes, etcetera. I did not spend a dime on glamorous underthings. I had to entice my love with just me.

I had been thinking for some time about what my friend had taught me and decided there was much logic and wisdom in her words. So, after a time, I changed my postulate about older men. Younger men could be more fun. I began to notice how many more widows there were than widowers—that somehow nature did not make a man to survive as well as a woman. Furthermore, when two people love each other they are seldom the same age, and it seems much better for the woman to be older. Just look around and observe: an older wife is seldom a partner in an unhappy marriage.

The great moment when I met Turnley came so quiet and unexpected. I had just returned home from a two weeks' absence. Family and friends were gathered in the living room, when this strange, beautiful young man came in, as if he lived there, and joined the group. Everyone seemed to know him, except me but actually, I was the only one who really knew him. I will never forget my exact thoughts the minute he walked in. "There is my man at last." I was so sure, I would have married him at once without the slightest doubt. I forgot all about making no compromise with marriage and such trivial things as name, job position, money, family or reputation.

But Turnley didn't share my enthusiasm. He didn't want any part of me, but there was an attraction because he went into a frenzy of dating every girl he could, except me. A little thing like that didn't worry me at all. The big thing was that I had found my man; the rest was just detail. So I paid no attention to him, except to make plans for my conquest. He was a big fish, born under the sign Pisces. He was six feet, one and three-quarters inches tall, fair, grey eyes, attractive and lovable. Such a wonderful fish to hook. After we were married, I told him what hussy tricks I had used to get him. From then on, he used to sing a little song to me: "Once you're hooked, your goose is cooked."

Enough of this interlude and nonsense. I am eager to start the story of our hectic and not-so-smooth romance.

4

Our Rugged & Rough Romance

During the next three months, I saw a lot of Turnley because in a small town, restaurant food was deplorable. Outsiders who had employment there always made a big pitch to get food at one of the private homes with the reputation of putting out good food. Turnley had already made his deal before I came home. We paid no attention to each other, but change seems to be the order of life.

Catharine planned a picnic trip to the beach and invited Turnley to go along and do the driving. The ocean was well over a hundred miles away. The trip was delightful; everything was pleasant dignity, Turnley keeping both hands on the steering wheel. But I had a little ace in the hole in the form of a new, bright red bathing suit. When I came on the beach everything suddenly changed. I was in his arms during all the time we were in the surf. On the drive home you could hardly call it pleasant dignity. Turnley never used but one arm. We didn't pay any attention to the family in the back seat. I felt happy and contented that my search was over.

Turnley was still nervous; he vaguely knew me from the past and was frightened. A few days later, in the evening after supper, he seemed upset and restless. I asked what was bothering him, as he was looking at his watch every few minutes. He explained that a friend had insisted on him meeting a certain girl, and he had to watch the time. I didn't let him know how much this upset me.

He took off to keep his date. I knew that some way, somehow, I must pull a rabbit out of the hat, so to speak, to make
a believer out of him. I sat on the porch and concentrated.
If I could only produce an eligible man quickly. Sure enough,
luck was with me.

Frank, a young man school teacher, single, attractive and
visiting his brother who was a close friend of the family,
came driving down the street alone. I grabbed the opportunity, went into the middle of the street, held up one arm
and he had to either stop or run over me. He stopped. I
simply got in his car and said, "Now, let's go places." Frank
seemed surprised but rose to the occasion. I continued to
play my role; I made no passes at him or anything that definite, but managed to give the vague impression that I was
quite a hussy. Fortunately, he made no passes at me. He
could have been slightly in shock. But he did begin to show
me a little disrespect which didn't bother me in the least as
I was playing for big stakes: my love!

When Frank and I were parked in front of the house,
Turnley drove by and saw us. I was radiantly delighted.
That's all I wanted. After this incident our romance seemed
to be on a firmer basis. I was so wrong; it wasn't firm at all,
just pure mush.

One evening we were riding around, always in his arms,
when he dug up Nancy and sprung her on me. He shocked
me when he said, "I would be the happiest man in the world
if I could make her my wife." Somehow, I handled the shock
and remained calm. It seems he had known Nancy since they
were about four or five years of age. As little children, he
thought she was the sweetest little girl. The thought may
have been implanted in their minds that when they grew
up, they would be sweethearts because, when they grew up,
they tried to work up some kind of romance, but they could
never get beyond the luke-warm stage.

I could hardly believe it was me talking when I heard my voice telling him that if he really wanted her so much, I would do all in my power to help him get her. That was my higher self speaking. But the lower self thought, "Damn you anyway, it will serve you right to get her." I had seen her photograph which was the image of a selfish, spoiled person. "I will make sure you get her." This incident had me fed up and cold.

The next evening Turnley was with me as usual, holding me tightly, when he asked me what I thought was the best way to go about winning Nancy. I told him I didn't think he would have the slightest trouble, but since he was not with her, it might be a good idea to write her a love letter and ask her if she would become his wife. He then wanted me to dictate every little detail. I told him it was his love affair, and the letter should come from his heart. If he truly loved her, that should be easy.

The next day he came in looking ghastly, like the cat that had swallowed the canary. He seemed about to collapse until he got his arms around me and said, "I am engaged." I replied, "How could you when you just wrote the letter last night?" He then explained that he just couldn't write a letter that sounded right. He tore up one letter after another. At 1:00 A.M. he called her long distance and bluntly asked her if she would marry him, and sleepy as she was, she said, "Yes." He told her he would see her in two weeks when he took his vacation.

I gently took his arms from around me and said, "Turnley, you and I have had a nice little flirtation. I have enjoyed it very much, but now that you are engaged, you are just a tame cat around here from now on."

Poor mixed up darling. What great lengths he would go to just to avoid life with me. His feelings were very hurt by my stand. I didn't see him for several days. He never mentioned Nancy again, but I sure did and kept on asking if he had written to her since that wild telephone call. I could never get him to communicate with her. He just said that it was not necessary, that he had told her he would see her when he took his vacation. I said, "Not necessary? I think it is mandatory that you write to her. Remember you accepted my offer to help you win her. I am going to see that you get her." Turnley was living hard during these days. I was gentle and kind but kept him at arm's length.

Finally the evening came when he was to take the all-night drive to see her and other friends. I fixed a good supply of food, hot coffee, even a bottle of wine. The next problem was getting him started. He just would not take off. I kept telling him about the long drive ahead. When he finally left, he managed to kiss me by kissing all the family first. He told me later he still didn't leave for a couple of hours, just sat in his room, deeply heartsick.

We didn't hear from him while he was away. On the day he was to return, Catharine suggested I should not be around so I planned a shopping trip to the city with friends. When I returned late (on purpose), Turnley was waiting for me. He jumped up and took both my hands in his and began telling me all about the wonderful trip he had, going from one happy incident to another and, suddenly, without changing his voice said, "and everything is off between Nancy and me." Still holding my hands I answered with great joy and said, "Good." I was caught off balance, as he had planned. But then I added in mock distress, "Oh, I mean I am so sorry." We both had a good laugh still holding hands. In fact, we went all through our life holding hands. I never again had a moment's worry or doubt where another woman was concerned. The things foolish people will go through for love, or to avoid it. A later chapter will add a big light on why it had to be this way.

There was another completely unexpected incident. This time the shoe was on the other foot. A telegram came from Bill saying he was coming for a few days' visit and for me to meet his train. His sixth sense must have been working, but a little late. My sixth sense told me he was going to suggest we stop fooling around and get married. I was too deeply fond of Bill to let him commit himself when I could not accept him. So, I decided to tell him as soon as I got him off the train that I had found the man I expected to marry. I did just this but he didn't seem surprised or upset.

An aunt was also visiting, an occult student, the only other one in the family beside me. Catharine and I planned a lovely dinner party but Turnley was very upset and declined to come to the party. I had a talk with him and asked if he would be proud of himself to run away in such a crisis. I told him that I would not be proud of him if he didn't come, that high grade people did not run away from unpleasant situations, but, of course, for him to do as he pleased. He didn't tell me what he was going to do.

He made it in a big way. We were all assembled on the piazza before dinner when Turnley drove up, proud and assured. His azure blue coupe had been washed and shined. He was dressed in his best light Palm Beach suit and his special white broadcloth shirt that looked like silk. I felt so proud and happy. It was a hot July evening and Turnley wanted a cold drink of water. I went with him to get it and put my arms around him and told him I did not love any one in the world but him.

The dinner was a delightful success. The most stimulating and unusual conversation floated around the table. We must have had numbers of invisible guests along with excellent food. Turnley said at that dinner he felt like the richest man in the world, because I had chosen him when a very wealthy man had loved me for years.

The rough times were over and we started making plans for our wedding. I wanted a very simple church wedding, no attendants and no one to give me away. I have always thought that marriage only concerned two people. Turnley wanted so many out-of-town guests. His plans would cost a lot of money, and the depression was on. He said he only expected to be married once in his life, and he wanted the world to know about it. So, I began to help Turnley plan a bigger and bigger wedding. Finally it dawned on him that things were getting a little out of hand.

Turnley insisted on me meeting his family before we were married. We had to make the trip over the weekend. The plans got a little mixed up. He wrote a letter to his parents giving the date we were coming. Then a little later he wrote another letter saying we couldn't get away at the time and would come later. Then he found we could come as first planned, but there was not time enough to write another letter. I suggested we call long distance. I didn't think he should bring a strange girl to his mother without notice but Turnley insisted his mother would know and be ready for us. He said he had never gone home unexpectedly that his mother didn't know and have all in readiness. He kept telling me not to worry about it. Could it be coincidence that my mother-in-law to be was telepathic?

We drove all afternoon and reached his grandparents' farm home about 9:00 P.M. They were very lovable people. The old farm and home had been in the family for generations and Turnley loved the place and his grandparents so much. He told me that as a boy, he used to dream about the time he would take his wife there and she would love it just as he did.

The next day we drove to his parents' home. I met my adored little mother-in-law. She was a tiny woman, never weighed more than 100 pounds. But she was potent and could do most anything, was afraid of nothing but thunder storms and fresh air. She loved everybody and everything, especially flowers, growing things and me. There was never anything but harmony and understanding between us. We had her until she was past eighty-two. On her last visit, I had the feeling we would not have her much longer. So I went in the yard with her and dug up shrubbery, plants, flowers, everything I could find. She was a little surprised at my burst of generosity. The car was packed with greenery. The last look I had of her, she was surrounded with the things she loved. She looked so happy as they drove away. I always thought she didn't know what I knew, but now I know better. She did know; she left us shortly after.

Now, back to that first visit. Mother was fussing about her family not believing her in the things she told them. When Dad got the letter saying we were not coming, he went on a little business trip. She begged him not to go, that we were coming, she knew it, but he went anyway. She proved her point by making a big fresh coconut white cake. God bless her now and always.

I remember Turnley and I were decorating the family Christmas tree. A warm, contented surge came over me as I thought I would never be lonely again on Christmas, because I would always have my love by my side.

We were married in January. It was a lovely simple church wedding with no attendants and no one to give me away. Turnley said he found out what best men were for. After getting dressed, he sat in his room and felt so desolate and disturbed. He didn't know why. If only he had a close friend standing by. He decided everything would be alright if he could just see me then, so he came right over. He was told he couldn't see the bride yet, but he demanded to see me. I had not finished dressing, but slipped on a robe and went to see about Turnley. He quieted down at once and was happy and confident again. I finished dressing and we spent the rest of the time together.

Big preparations for the wedding dinner were under way in the kitchen. We just gazed at each other until it was time to go to the church for the 5:00 P.M. ceremony. We walked down that middle aisle triumphant and radiant. A few minutes after the minister started reading the service, I went into violent shakes. You couldn't call it a tremble. It was heavy. Turnley had to grab me with both arms and hold me tightly for the rest of the service. I felt humiliated to have this happen before a church packed with friends, but it was a comfort to know my love would take care of me in any crisis.

We had a happy life together. There was never the slightest question of another woman. He always insisted he loved me more than I loved him. I always stood firm on the opposite. To prove his point, he said he was never under the impression that he had ever loved any woman except me. But I had several serious love affairs; about this my readers will smile with me about his impressions.

We had to go through several severe crises and struggles, but always came through loving each other and winning over all obstacles. As the song says, "I reached for your hand, it was always there." We had nearly forty-one years together. Near the end, I asked him again, "Who loves who the most?" He drew me to him and said, "Honey it's a draw." His loss was a crushing sorrow. I will not dwell on it further here, but the great love I have always had for God sustained me even in this, giving me strength and understanding.

Out of the great loss and with God's constant love and guidance, I have been privileged to write a strange, unusual, revealing book that will shake and interest my readers to the depths of their being. Nothing has been written from memory. I have had to relive it in order to give exact details.

Every word is true. The data that I did not live are given straight from the Divine source, word for word as received.

A little item of interest. When studying astrology, our teacher mentioned to the girls that when they were married, to be sure and have Venus in the seventh house of marriage, even if you must have the ceremony in the middle of the night. I wondered where Venus was when my marriage took place so a chart was erected for the exact time. Venus was in close conjunction with the Sun in Aquarius in the seventh house and perfectly aspected. Could this be coincidence? Much study and observation has satisfied me that there is no coincidence. We live in an orderly planned life. Nothing happens by chance or accident.

5

Significant Data

There was a series of incidents on a chain similar in nature which was the result of a heavy basic incident that happened before birth, which was keyed in at the age of three years.

I was never much of a baby or a child. Living with adults there was little experience with children. I walked and talked at about ten months. Shortly after I took care of my personal needs, such as a drink of water and the potty. This seemed natural as it should be. Lily was my mother. The servants called her Miss Lily, but Pappa and family said Lily. She was very beautiful and gracious and believed in prenatal influence. She studied all manner of things, went to concerts, dramas, etc., but Shakespeare was the love of her life. She hated mathematics, but worked hard at it, so I have always hated numbers and math. Before three, I managed to get her volume of Shakespeare on a wide window sill. It was hard to do, but so easy to give it the old heave-ho out of the window. I was lonely and did not have enough of Lily's time and attention. I just tried to handle my first problem.

I had a happy incident before three. Lily was shopping when I saw a miniature piano. It was real. I looked at it transfixed, and slowly moved to put out a finger to touch a note. The sound thrilled me through and through. Gradually I touched other notes with more joy. Later Lily came to take me home. I told her very firmly I would not leave the piano.

She said it was getting late and the store would soon close. I told her that didn't make any difference to me. She then told me about being locked up in the dark and all alone. "No, I will not be alone, I will have the piano." Finally, in desperation she promised to have a piano delivered to me if I would come with her now. Being thoroughly reasonable I agreed to go with her. A few days later my joy turned to disgust. When a miserable little child's toy piano was given me. I pitched it away and never looked at it again. I never saw another piano until I was nine years of age. Pappa had agreed to store it in his home for a few months. I rolled over and over in my joy. I was soon taking piano lessons. Pappa and I were both thrilled when I played, "Little Wee fingers" a short time later at a recital.

I now relate the incident at three years that nearly wrecked my life, and keyed in the series of incidents that caused heavy aberrations on my sex life. My beautiful, blessed mother loved me very dearly, and would never knowingly bring any harm to me. She probably had her full share of engrams and was sick on the subject of sex. How strange that man's greatest and most creative power comes from love and sex but it is also the more aberrated from lack of understanding.

Lily and I were visiting cousins, one morning while the maid was dressing James, my four year old cousin. I noticed something peculiar about his body. I went closer to get a good look. I thought I had made a mistake—no, he was different. I took off calling Lily. I thought she would give me an explanation. I told her I had made a startling discovery. (Yes, those were the exact words.) She then asked, "How do you know?" I answered truthfully and said I know because I had looked. Then, she lost all contact with reason or sense of reality and kept asking me why I looked. I kept on telling her. She began spanking me harder all the time.

Finally, I said, "Lily, if you tell me what you want me to say, I will say it." No answer, just soul torturing words that were occluded until many years later. I was in heavy shock by this time. My whole world had collapsed by just looking. I had wrecked everything I loved. It is a wonder that I did not go blind.

After Dianetic processing the words were recovered and the entire story in bits. The words were: "I would rather God take you from me now than have you grow up to be a bad woman." Remember these words. They are the key and play an important role in this story.

At six there was another sex incident. Some boys had a tent in the backyard. A boy came to me and said, "We have candy." He wanted me to have some. I liked candy so I hurried to the tent. When I reached the entrance I saw, (looked) at this twelve year old boy who was exposed. I backed away shocked and ran as fast as I could. You can be sure I never told anyone about it until now. I am writing about it for the world to read. It is a simple, uninteresting incident alone, but fastened to this chain it becomes significant. They piled up from thirteen to fifteen. At four, I lost my adored Lily. Her death was a crushing blow to me. I was a very bright and normal child before the looking incident and then the loss of Lily put me into a deep state of apathy that lasted for years. I was past fifty before I stopped grieving for her.

I can remember so clearly as she stood on the steps to kiss me goodby, and as she was ready to get in the carriage to leave, I held on so tightly and begged her not to leave me.

Two years later Pappa married Catharine, one of Lily's younger sisters, and we left the south to live in Indiana. When thirteen we were visiting other cousins in Texas. Tom, the older boy was just my age. A darling boy, but a big tease. We had just arrived and getting acquainted again.

Tom said, "Cousin Catharine, would you like to see how I kiss a pretty girl?" After a yes answer, Tom stepped on the rocker and the chair went way back with me and my dignity on it. Then he firmly planted a kiss on my cheek. I was shocked, but mostly surprised. I might have enjoyed the joke if the others had not laughed so long and hard. Teasing was not the main trouble I had with Tom. It was so many boy, friends who hung around. As long as we were playing, run, ning around and whooping it up in the yard, I thought boys were great, but I liked to take quiet walks by myself. These boys would then gang up on me and follow at a distance wherever I went. When I turned around they gave me a dying cat look. I just couldn't stand that. I begged them to stop following me. No answer. Only dumb looks. Then I tried paying no attention to them. That did not work either. They were always there. I did not know why, but this gave me an uncomfortable feeling that something was wrong. I felt degraded and humiliated. This did not last long, because the visit was soon over, but the memory was carried over when I was fourteen and fifteen.

We lived near a park where there were Sunday band concerts. I just loved crowds, activity and music, but felt sick again when groups of boys ganged up on me exactly as it had been in Texas, except I didn't know the boys this time. I was never alone in the park. My younger sister and another girl were always together. I just couldn't give up the band concert, so I did the next best thing and blocked them out of my consciousness. A little later Catherine was shocked when my sister mentioned casually, "I never saw the like of how Marie Louise breeds boys in the park by the hun, dreds." My sister was inclined to exaggerate. Catherine then asked, "What does Marie Louise do about it?" Her answer was, "Nothing at all. She acts like she doesn't even know they are there."

I suddenly developed a beautiful voice, not long before fourteen. I informed my father at once that I was going to be a prima donna. He laughed and said, "Don't you know you must have a voice to be a prima donna?" I answered, "I have the voice, just listen to this." I opened my mouth and let some lovely soprano tones float out. Papa said afterwards, "You opened your mouth and let out some loud squawks." I told Papa I needed a voice teacher. He agreed to pay for the lessons if I could find a teacher. I found the teacher by asking everybody I contacted if they could tell me where I could find a voice teacher. Finally it payed off. I was told to contact a certain woman who was a patron of the arts, and she could tell me anything I wanted to know. She did not live very far from me and I got the information. I did not waste any time before I was working hard with my teacher. During the third lesson I felt deep despair and felt I could never handle it. This lasted only for one lesson. Then, everything cleared up. Hearing the word "prima donna" for the first time caused goose pimples to come all over me, but was deeply fascinating. Then I suddenly had a beautiful voice with no idea of how I got it. The word "prima donna" keyed in the voice. In the early days my teacher disgusted me with silly little songs she gave me. I remember "Baby's Boats A Silver Moon" and "Dear Jerushy." I humored her for a little while, then told her I was not interested in those silly little songs. It was not my idea of what I would like to sing. She then asked me what kind of song I had in mind. I told her, "Bartlett's 'A Dream.'" She took a fit and told me that was a hundred times too difficult for me. I told her I couldn't see anything difficult about it, that I had been singing that and numbers of other beautiful songs with perfect ease and beauty. Anyway, she didn't palm off any more silly, childish songs on me.

Grand opera was my goal then. It was life and heaven to

me. I liked boys fine as I did everyone else, so long as it was in groups, but when I saw that certain gleam in the male eye it made me sick all over. So, I refused all dates. When Catherine said we could not date any boys who smoked cigarettes, my sister was very upset. I was delighted as it gave me an excuse not to date.

I developed very beautifully, very happy, radiant and enthusiastic, singing most of the time, but deep down I was worried. I knew I was not normal where boys were concerned. After much thought I tried to change and overcome this condition. So, I dated a very nice young man at seventeen years of age. The boy was twenty-one. We had about three dates and I began to feel like I was perfectly normal until he brought me home after our fourth date. As Frank said goodnight he asked to kiss me. I said in no uncertain voice, certainly not. The poor boy was timid but nature is not, and he came a little closer and said, "Oh, please!" That did it, and I asked if he had gone crazy and added, "Don't you ever speak to me again." I went upstairs to Catherine. I should have gone to Papa, but thought he would not understand how serious it was. I felt so depressed, just like I was already a bad woman. Catherine didn't help matters. She just put her arm around my shoulders and said, "Don't be upset, you acted as any well bred young lady should." This remark is significant. We will reveal a little later just why she had this attitude. Catherine plays a strong role in a past life. I was upset over Frank for two reasons. My abnormality and the useless hurt I had given a very nice young man. I have wished many times I could undo the damage to him. No more dates or incidents until I was nineteen.

By this time I was a finished concert singer. We moved to a large cultural city as Papa wanted me to have more advantages. I attended open house Sunday gatherings held by a couple who were patrons of the musical arts. It was there I met a brilliant concert violinist of Russian birth. He was also a doctor. He called at my home at once. Catherine was worried about this, but everyone seemed to know all about my visitor, and were high in their praises that he had an excellent reputation, belonged to the best club and was lionized by the musical and cultural elite of the city. Catherine was worried and wanted to break it up. Everyone advised her not to object because that would deny me many pleasant musical and social contacts. My father received a letter from the admirer stating he admired his daughter very much and would like his permission to court her. Also, he would like Papa to call at his office and he would answer any questions he wished to ask. Papa felt like he had a hot potato and didn't know what to do with it. He would not answer the letter so I had to explain the situation as best I could. I continued to see him for a number of weeks. He got me a number of concert engagements along with him. He spent money on me like it was water. Next to music he loved dancing more than anything. Catherine saw an opportunity and said, "No public dances—only if they were private." This seemed like a large obstacle. But love usually finds a way and he did. He had an invitation to a rare thing, a private dance. The only condition was that he had to take another girl to this dance. I told him that this was perfectly alright. We went to the dance. Catherine lost that round. The orchestra was very poor and after the first dance, he suggested there was an orchestra on the main floor that was tops. He gave me a pleading look and said, "Couldn't we go downstairs to dance?" A little crack of light dawned on me and I said happily, "Oh yes, let's do." The music was superb. The atmosphere and service all that could be desired, besides I had a snug little feeling of satisfaction that I had disobeyed Catherine, which gave me a good sense of freedom which belonged to me. I had never danced with such a good dancer. With his strong

lead I could do any kind of dancing. A small item. My partner ordered the most wonderful food. Before I could take
more than a few bites the orchestra started up again and he
couldn't stand it. With gusto he would say, "Let's dance
this one." This kept up all evening. When this was over I
had looked at a lot of good food, but had little chance of
eating it, and I was plain hungry. We did make it back to
the private dance before it was over, so he could take his
date home, along with me.

After a while he started talking about looking at apart-
ments. This made me sick, but he seemed to be very understanding and sensitive to pick up my moods or aberration.
But I was trying very hard. I liked him and knew he was a
top human being. He was patient and handled me with kid
gloves. I know this doesn't sound like a sex incident on the
chain, just wait. The little demon was coming. One evening
after returning from a date, the family had retired. We were
alone in the living room. He talked about great artists. I
loved that. Getting closer all the time, he continued, "The
truly great artist, one who stands way out above others actually has just gone one little notch beyond the good artist,
but there were so few that could make the last little grade."
I know now what he was talking about. That last little grade
is purely spiritual power and has nothing to do with the
physical, but it does clothe artistry with divine ecstacy and
beauty. It is a pure essence of spirit which is closely tied to
art. With my mind on high art I was lifted above the ordinary vibrations of thought. My friend was closer to me
now and leaned over and gently placed a tender little kiss
on my lips. There was no passion which I knew nothing
about. I felt very good about it. I wanted so much to be
normal.

But my friend just would not leave. I was tired, but patient. Finally I got him to the front door, and no further. He

hung on and on. Love is so wonderful. I blush to think I didn't appreciate it then. I was too young and inexperienced for it to penetrate the sex block. Finally in desperation I said, "Oh, do run along!" He left quickly and I saw him only once after that. A casual meeting, pleasant but changed, but I have never forgotten him. I realize I would have been happy with him.

The next day I told Catherine exactly what had happened about the kiss. She pumped it up beyond any resemblance to truth. She was sarcastic and treated me as some kind of an outcast. She went too far and I became very angry. I was aberrated on sex, but I was not dumb, so I had a talk with my father and told him I was leaving home, which had become unbearable to me. Papa took me on his lap, which was extreme action for my dignified Papa. I explained everything to him. He told me I didn't have to leave home, he could promise me there would be changes and quickly. I don't know what he said to Catherine, but she changed at once, and was all sweetness, but as time went on she lost control over me. She became more evil. In fact, the most evil thing in my life. Only recently I found out the part she played in the past life, which this story will explain and reveal at the right time.

A little later on I signed a contract to go on my first tour. Catherine some way prevailed on Papa to keep me off the stage. In this respect I was not at all aberrated. I told Papa I would remain an obedient daughter until I was twenty-one, but on that very day I was taking off. I told him I didn't think parents had the right to dictate their child's life after twenty-one, or what profession they chose to follow. Papa said, "Marie Louise, you are so right, you need not wait until you are twenty-one. You are free to go at any time you wish and I will help you all I can." I sure had a wonderful father. There was always love and harmony between us. The next incident on the chain came when I was twenty-one. I met a man, a real estate developer who did business with Papa. After we met he called at our home every day or so and was most charming and entertaining to the family. He was the first man who ever attracted me. I thought I would enjoy his company very much, and would like to see more of him. Catherine was really worried. She was going to do all in her power to keep any man from coming near me. She sure had a big job, but she was determined.

I was talking to Allen out in the front yard. He was visiting his brother, who lived next door. I blush with shame when I write that Catherine called out to me in a sharp tone of voice, "Marie Louise, come into the house this minute." I went in determined to have it out with her once and for all, when she played her trump card with the words, "I would rather see you dead and in your casket than to marry that man." Second mother and almost the same words that were so painful to me. There was nothing wrong with this man. He had a father he disliked and ran away from home at fifteen taking his younger brother with him. They always remained together. Allen was very clever and able with strong survival abilities. When I met him Papa said he was worth about fifty thousand dollars from real estate operations. He continued to contrive ways to meet me down town with the help of his sister-in-law. Catherine caught on to this and became a devil on the war path. I could have so easily told Allen I would be glad to meet him anywhere, and he was free to call for me at my home. Catherine told the sister-in-law that it nearly sent her crazy at the thought of my leaving home. That I was the light and joy of her life. Allen went to California and sold the balance of his subdivision to Papa. Shortly thereafter, he became a millionaire.

Getting away from Catherine, after signing a contract

for my first concert tour and assuming full responsibility for myself, was like a new birth. Through the analytical mind and other healthy conditions, the little demons of sex aberrations were gone for good. Or nearly so.

The next few years were the happiest of my life except I had so many heart aches in my love life. All this will be cleared up when we contact Grassini.

In the meantime, I still had Catherine. She went so far in her jealousy, that years later on our wedding night, when I went to get my bags and returned to the living room, she had her arms around Turnley's neck begging him not to take me away from her. She pleaded with him to leave me with her for just one more night. Turnley was embarrassed and told her he certainly would not. At this time Catherine didn't have the slightest control over me. I said, "Catherine, this is a matter neither you nor Turnley can control. I married him this evening, I am his wife and I am going with him. So, cut out the dramatics." After I married Turnley, what she called love turned to hate as time went on. What she had in place of love was transferred to Turnley. We were stuck with her. She didn't have the finances to live away from us. We had already lost my beloved Papa.

As always I prayed to God to make things right, and He sure did. Catherine met a man she admired, but he had a wife and four children in college. Once a year we heard from him at Christmas time. This was his habit with a large circle of friends. As an astrologer I had predicted that Catherine was going to be re-married. It was not wishful thinking. It was there to be read by any competent astrologer. This was in November. I said she would be re-married the last of May. Concerning this there was a humorous incident. We had a table of bridge to celebrate a psychic friend's birthday, who was forty-five and just happened to be a little bit pregnant. She read the cards for Catherine not knowing about my prediction, and told her she was going to be married. A few minutes later Catherine asked the card reader if she had a pattern for baby clothes. (Catherine's specialty was exquisite baby clothes.) My spinster friend said bluntly, "Why do you need a pattern for baby clothes?" Catherine said quickly, "Didn't you just hear the lady tell me I am going to be married?" Catherine was past sixty.

About two weeks later the letter came, the annual one, but a long one this time. At the finish he dropped his bomb. His wife had divorced him. Not the wife of the four children, she had died under surgery, but a much younger woman whom he had married. I felt the usual goose pimples and knew Catherine had her man and Turnley and I would be released.

Another little item. The romance had its ups and downs, and over a trifle Catherine became angry and broke the engagement for a few days. This made me sick and upset. With a cold cloth on my head and my feet in a pan of hot water, Catherine had a big laugh and said, "I had to nurse you through your love affairs, but I didn't think I would have to nurse you through mine, too." She was married May 30, as predicted.

I never read a chart on how I think an aspect will work out. I read the chart, make the predictions on chart and aspects alone, and that's as far as I go. On this prediction all my astrology friends thought I had gone off the deep end. They asked how in the world do you think she will find a man? My answer was, "I certainly do not know how. I have no idea of how or where, but come he will somehow— even if the heavens open up and just drop him down."

Catherine became more and more evil and shortly after her marriage she went out of my life forever. I hope all accounts are settled in full.

It has been necessary to bring in these sex incidents all on a chain, in order to give understanding of the purpose and plan of living. A belief that one life covers everything is nothing but utter confusion. We come to this Earth to have the necessary experience for evolvement. One life time is just like one day in school. We live then pass on into a spiritual plane, not the final and everlasting heaven. We are not ready for that now. There are no material considerations on this next plane. But—we must take a good look at the life just lived. Somehow the soul, or thetan is forced to honestly judge itself with critical perceptions. At this time a chance is given to make new postulates on the next life. The soul is free to choose good and higher evolvement, or just the opposite. The mystery is how any soul can choose evil over good. But as we say, smart people learn by their mistakes, but fools never learn.

This book could not have been written sooner than a year ago. It has taken a long, life time.

6

Several Interesting Psychic Experiences

At eighteen years of age I had my first exceptional experience. I had been introduced to a brilliant and magnetic criminal lawyer. I had only been with him twice when my visit was over, away from home. Several letters came. I was attracted to him, but he was twenty-five years older than I. His career was brilliant, he had never been known to have lost a case.

One evening shortly after my return home about eight in the evening, I suddenly looked out of the windows to the East. The moonlight was bright. I remarked to Catherine, "Oh, it is such a beautiful moonlight night. I would give anything if I could be with Gordon on a ship in the Chesapeake Bay." I lingered for a while, dreamily looking to the East. Two days later I received a letter from Gordon that started like this, quote, "It is a beautiful moonlight night on the deck of a ship on the Chesapeake Bay. I fancy telepathy is drawing you near me, dear. Let me know about this. It is nine P.M., with me and eight P.M., with you. Would to God you were with me."

At twenty I had a vision, during sleep, all in color, clear in every detail which has never faded from memory. I was singing a heavy operatic aria in a large opera house. It was at La Scala in Milan. Pictures of the interior looking from stage gave me instant recognition. There were so many balconies, one on top of the other and circular in shape. As I looked at the packed audience, I noticed the stage lighting was not very bright. As I sang the magnificent aria I had the feeling it was my greatest performance. I slowly worked to right front stage where I made my exit. The first second off stage I gave way to the most heart breaking sobs, the whole body was shaking and I could feel a little head piece bobbing up and down. The house was in a mad uproar, shouting and screaming, "Bravo." This outburst intensified the grief. This went on for some time, until I was pushed and urged back on stage to accept the ovation.

End of first part of vision.

Without waking I went into another vision quite different. I was happily married to a man several years younger, whom I did not see in this vision. It seems I had just had a son who was ten years old and playing with a big dog in the yard. I wanted to give him the name William, but he wanted the simple name of Jack. As I went back into the house and looked into a mirror I was surprised that I looked like a very young girl. We were in modest but comfortable circumstances and usually owned the lots on both sides of the home. My son has never been separated from big dogs, weighed nearly ten pounds at birth. At ten years of age he looked exactly like the vision. My father, my son and my grandson all had the firm name William.

Although the visions were as clear as crystal, my interpretations were off. I thought I was being offered whichever life I wanted. In spite of the sorrow I still wanted opera more than anything else. For several years there was a big conflict of wanting both opera and children, but couldn't have both. I had to make a choice, with each desire tugging at my soul, I finally decided I wanted love of a husband and children more than anything else. It was a very hard choice. I really had no choice from the visions. I had the opera career in the last past life and a husband and son in this life.

I married a man seven years younger. We had a deep love

for each other. I had the ten pound boy shortly after my thirty-fifth birthday. Three years later I started astrological study. When I was still a beginner, Anne Porter, our brilliant teacher, was reading from a chart on the board. She pointed out that the native had damaged his stomach and kidneys probably from heavy use of alcohol in the last life. Before that, the body was strong. She explained that the soul could not reincarnate with healthy organs it already had damaged. As I went home I pondered over this and wondered what I could have done to give me such an affliction in the sign Scorpio. I sure found out that very night while sleeping. I was looking into a kaleidoscope with a bright light at the other end. I saw scene after scene, each time the vision would scramble up and a new and clear one form. I saw myself as the opera singer, but what scandalous gal she was. I have had a lot of sorrow taking responsibility for *Jose*. As I looked I bowed my head in shame. But I am thankful I know the cause of the things that have happened to me. The vision even brought in the singer Grassini boarding a ship to sing a season of opera in South America. This just to keep the identity straight. In this book I am baring my soul to the world to bring you true data. I don't mind that at all if it opens new vistas of thought, knowledge and responsibility for others.

The contact with Houdini happened while I was in the hospital after a stroke and unconscious most of the time. The doctor gave my husband a big shock when he was told there was little hope for my recovery. But the doctor was wrong, as I had a one hundred percent recovery which a specialist said was very remarkable. Which only proves there are just two who control life and death. God and the being concerned. It happened during a short period of partial consciousness. The whole body was securely tied. It was a shock to see how my feet were hog-tied. I struggled hard to get loose when I heard a gentle voice tell me to be quiet as there was no way for me to get loose and I needed all my strength to get well. The voice continued by suggesting I relax and go back to sleep, whcih I did at once. When I woke up I was amazed to find I was perfectly free, which was used for the ordinary business of going to the bath room. All was fine until I started to get back in bed and then I collapsed. When I regained consciousness the room was full of nurses and people, including my husband and I sensed a lot of consternation, but no one talked except my husband and we never lost communication. No matter how much I was out I could always answer him with a yes or no. He said, "Honey, just hang on to that yes and no and we will make it." Turnley turned to me and said, "Marie Louise, how in the world did you get loose?" He said I held up one finger and said, "Houdini." I suppose everyone in that room settled down and accepted such a reasonable answer. They must have thought I was in a pitiful condition, but it was a true answer and I was free and never have been tied up since. I pondered for months just how did Houdini do it. Finally, one day I thought Houdini is dead and does not have a physical body. Then it flashed! I had a physical body and it was hog-tied. Only Houdini's body had died, but still had all his great genius and know-how, but with no body to turn loose. He still gets pleasure from turning bodies loose, but was too highly evolved to use his great gift unwisely.

I realize I have taken my readers on a big jump, but it is true that souls can occupy other bodies for short periods and by one soul's consent to another. The soul is so free and able to be anywhere instantly by thought alone. This is the one and only truth to explain how it happened. Believe me, he had to get into my body to free me. When he found me helpless and tied securely he was in business again. Besides, he and I are both Leos and in the theatrical profession.

Another great experience came after I had a strong desire to talk to some higher being from another planet. I talked this over with my husband and asked him to sit with me for more power. We sat in concentration for about three evenings when the first faint communication came to the effect that they were working on my body. The next evening everything came through clear and distinct. I was in contact. I asked, "Where are you?" The answer was, "On a distant planet not in your solar system, the name would mean nothing to you." As he started to continue I asked if he would speak to me in relays, giving me time to repeat it to Turnley, as otherwise the conversation would be silent, but perfectly clear and distinct. I said everything out loud, but repeated out loud what they gave me. I got a quick consent and we started, "As you know there are people on other planets much more highly evolved than on Earth. We want you to know just how we accomplish all this." Pause . . . repeat to Turney. "Everything we do is by the application of the principle of the love of God." Pause . . . repeat. I said, mentally, "I do not entirely understand, will you explain in more detail?" More pauses and relays to Turnley. But he told me whenever you see a hungry person or animal you feed them, or even a tree or growing plant you give it water or whatever it needs. I thought instantly, "My goodness, I have been doing that all my life." Quickly the answer, "Yes, we know you have been doing this all your life, but now we are asking you to do it a little differently." Truly thoughts are things of great power. In the future when you do anything for people or things, just say mentally, "The love of God flows through me to you."

I was so grateful for the contact and message, but regret to say I slipped more and more due to the heavy responsibilities of the material world, which was wrong. There is nothing more important than spiritual responsibilities. Several years passed and I began to feel the pull that I had neglected to use a gem given to me. I quickly contacted the original source again, and said how sorry I was for the neglect. In the future, I would make a bigger effort to avail myself of the wisdom it contained. It was then explained that it was given because it is packed with power, and they wanted me to have it. Perhaps they knew I would share it with the world for those who could tune in. I find by use that it is packed with power. In most everything I do now, the love of God flows freely. I believe the magic is in the Trinity used as a flow from God to you for the nature of love does flow. Scientology has recently discovered that their most powerful processes are the triple flows.

Here is another experience that is worthy of a place in this book. I had a clear communication that I would soon see a picture of my past body. I told my husband about this at once. We discussed and wondered how this could possibly happen, where and how could such a photograph be given. We did not doubt that it would happen, and I would certainly recognize a body I had lived in for a life time. I had learned by experience not to doubt anything received from beyond the conscious mind. So I pondered deeply. But no further communication until a few weeks later when Turnley brought in the Sunday papers and gave me the arts and letters section and took the sports page for himself. I was glancing casually over the account about the new art museum and certain valuable art pieces that had been loaned to the museum which were on display. Before I could read any more my attention was drawn to the picture of a woman. I took another look and the goose pimples popped out all over, and the emotions went wild when I fully realized in the next few seconds it was me. It would be hard to describe the reactions. I did not say a word to my husband sitting so close to me reading the sports page. I threw the paper down on the pile with the other papers. I quieted down and tried to let reason prevail. The next morning at the first little dawn of consciousness I heard a gentle voice say, "That is your picture." Presumably my higher spiritual or theta self. So I went to the pile of newspapers and found the article, read it slowly and carefully. The portrait was named Carmen. It was painted about the turn of the century by a famous American artist. The name Carmen was significant because the life of Grassini had been so much like the character and personality portrayed in the role of Carmen many years after Grassini's time. Georges Bizet, composer of Carmen, knew all about the career and life of Grassini; so it would seem that he composed the greatest opera of all time based on her character and personality. Also, the portrait artist who painted Carmen which was a perfect likeness of Grassini, made from a sketch years earlier in Turkish costume. This could not be a coincidence. The artist had to know the facts about the real living grand opera singer and the fictitious character of Carmen. Both images were alike in that they both had many lovers, one right after another. Both had great power of attraction for men. He also had to get a picture of Grassini who was real.

The opera Carmen is rated above all others and has been produced much more than any other opera. Bizet knew in his heart and soul that he had been privileged to compose a great masterpiece, but when it was first produced in Paris it was a dismal failure and he died of a broken heart.

The opera is so great and complex, even highly trained opera lovers could not grasp the enormity of it at the first hearing. Each time the opera is heard, more and more is revealed to the consciousness. The wild gypsy music is strong and thrilling, but the deep undertones of tragic beauty keep building up all through the opera, along with the exciting gypsy theme. Both gaining power to grip the emotions. I do not know of this quality in any other opera. Only the greatest geniuses could have accomplished it.

No wonder those who heard it first were confused and uncertain. They could not grasp much of its power and greatness, but it sure grew on them later.

Whenever I hear Carmen I sob through much of it, but after the performance is over and I get back to present time, there is joy and radiance just like I had swallowed a whole bottle of vitamins. I was very sure, but just for the fun of it at the next opportunity, I had the picture with me on the EMeter. I think the auditor thought she was just going through the test because I asked for it. But she jumped up with excitement and surprise and said, "It reads."

Now—leaving heavy psychic experience, we proceed to some lighter and more amusing incidents.

My husband was a football player. He loved all sports and had dreamed for years how much pleasure he would have taking his future wife to the games.

After we were married he tried it once. I didn't know the first thing about the game. He tried to explain the game to me. I didn't get the hang of it quickly and thought he was very vague. Anyway, he never took me to another game. I was sorry about this and after a number of years it suddenly dawned on me there was another way to amuse him. I felt if the desire was strong enough I could tell him who was going to win. I concentrated on it and was granted the power to know what team was going to win. I never told him wrong and we were both delighted but money could never play a part in this.

Once he came in depressed that his university was in bad condition. There were nothing but untried sophomores to start the season. Instantly it flashed in my mind and I said, "What do you mean by nothing but sophomores?" "You are going to get a surprise about how good they are." "They will win most of their games!"

I never did understand anything about the game, but as a team won a game, Turnley would look at me and say, "I just don't know how you do it!" I don't know how I do it either, except I am clearly told. Once he came in and suddenly asked me what team would win a certain game. I told him, "I don't know, I have not been told." But in that instant I was told so I quickly told him what team would win. We both got such a thrill out of these experiences.

There is one more I would like to mention. We were watching the televised account of the third and last race. It was for the triple crown. The first one, the Kentucky Derby the second one, Pimlico, and this third and last race was at Saratoga, New York. The big favorite was the horse that had easily won the first two races. The experts felt sure this horse could win the triple crown. We listened to more of the experts' opinions on how sure they were that this horse would win again.

I loved and understood horse races, but even in this I didn't know what horse was going to win unless I was told. Suddenly I said, "Why, Turnley, this horse will not even be in the money." He came in fourth, not in the money.

I of myself in these matters know nothing beyond the physical evidence. I do know these psychic revelations are not thought out with the analytical mind. They come suddenly, but clear and concise. I can tell you a little of how the psychic faculty is developed. We all have it in a latent state. God intended man to know or have psychic abilities. First there must be a great love for God and his creation, and to be in tune with the universe. Next, they must be an ardent seeker after truth. The more one deviates from truth, the more confused they become and the less they know.

Truth is built upon a firm, precious and wonderful foundation.

7

Fantastic Abilities of the Soul

The first fact should be established that you are the immortal soul. You have always lived and always will. There is nothing you do not know. You were created to be one with God. At this point there is a separation of destinies because of the two great immutable laws by which man must live and know. Evolvement and free will. God could have created souls to be absolutely perfect. Without these great laws, man would be more or less the same as His creation of the animal world, governed by implanted instinct.

Evidently God did not wish it to be that way which would bore Him and be futile and useless. He had far greater plans for man. Even God must have the understanding love of His Creations who were created in His image with the final result of the God Hood of man equal even to God. Example of this is Jesus Christ, son of God, who was one or equal to God.

I wonder how many people give little or no thought to God. How many go to God only if they need help desperately? How many pray regularly with lip service given by rote? How many pray to God constantly for help, guidance and for the sheer love and joy of close contact with Him?

An interesting fact came to me from a great physician who used electronics as a tool which easily detected cancer and all sources of body illnesses, and also to cure unless the body was so far gone the soul had already rejected it. He started to do some serious thinking when he discovered the very instant the soul left the body, every living germ or bacteria in the body had vanished. No life of any kind could be in a body which had been vacated by the soul. The doctor did not do any bedside palaver. He worked from his home and office with only electronic instruments of his own invention and making which measured and contacted everything in the body. He said it gave him the most peculiar feeling of awe while in close contact with a very sick body, and suddenly all went dead. He could get no response from the germs, disease or anything in the body. All was dead— nothing left but a decaying little mass chemical matter.

The natural life of a physical body is about ten times its maturity. The animal kingdom all live this long except for accidents or violent death, because they do not have much free will. Everything is controlled by instinct. They do not carry any load of aberrations because they are as God intended them to be.

If man lived his natural physical span of life, it would be for 130 to 150 years. Due to unbelief and abuse of free will, things get badly messed.

There is much evidence the soul does not reject a body unless it becomes so unknowing and confused it believes it has no power of any kind, then, death is a natural release. A being does not die unless it has lost all contact with joy and the ability to solve problems. This concept can only come from the negative mortal mind. Not ever from the gloriously alive soul or thetan.

Remember the words, "The last enemy to be overcome is death." But since there has been misunderstanding concerning the soul, we can accept a new concept better with a new name. Ron Hubbard, founder and developer of Dianetics and Scientology, used the words theta and thetan from the Greek symbols, meaning thought and spirit. You are the thetan who handles theta.

We are dealing with three levels of mind. The lower

mind does not compute. It is a negative, reactive response there to safeguard physical survival in case of severe injury or danger when the more delicate and sensitive analytical mind usually shuts off. The analytical mind covers the great in-between connecting the other two levels. It makes all the computations and never makes a mistake unless fed wrong data from the reactive mind. It is the only route to the higher mind of spirit.

This third level is where theta operates, and the whole life is either run badly or good. It is here the thetan is free and able to use its vast powers, if not downgraded through much false attraction to evil.

The average person does not use much of the analytical computation, much less computations from the third level. Many think the five senses are adequate. So all beings are not in the same condition of evolvement. The variations are great, as the power is potential and must be developed by recognition and use.

If you are alive, you can make up spiritually and claim anything the mind can conceive. That is why the tender, merciful God put guide posts all along the path of evolvement. The foundation of these guide posts are in His simple Commandments—certainly not for God's pleasure or protection—only to help His evolving creations. The two great Commandments, "Love thy God with all thy strength of thy mind and thy soul, and your fellow man as thyself." These were given to serve as stable datum until theta is fully awake and knows how to go straight to the source.

It is established knowledge that most people use only one-tenth of their mental and spiritual capacity. The nine-tenths are there alright but solidly frozen. Alive but inactive. This frozen part is the mind and abilities of theta and all its vast powers. Just think about what priceless material has been going to waste, waiting for eager beaver probers to get busy and claim that lucious big nine-tenths. This is our birthright and promises from God that there are ways we can thaw the frozen nine-tenths and claim the glorious big frozen part, for now and forever. Just as we exercise weak muscles to strengthen them, so we work to strengthen spiritual muscles and fiber.

Ron Hubbard has spent most of his life devising means and processes by which this can be accomplished. The auditors who run the processes are able and highly trained, but expensive. The cost is about $30.00 per hour and worth every bit it costs. The Hubbard foundation in Los Angeles is headquarters in this Country. The address is 916 South Westlake St., Los Angeles, California 90006.

But this is written for the vast majority who must do it themselves, through the grace of God.

To know about God and His laws there is no higher source than the infallible words and teaching of Jesus Christ. Almost every home has a bible where his precious words can be read at any time. He gave his life to bring you to the truth. Not because it was necessary for Him to die, but in order for His death to fully reveal to the world, *His Life*. How much, Oh God, have we cherished those words that could bring peace, joy and a higher civilization for all? The time is soon coming when even the love of God will not tolerate the gross stupidity of man. Twenty-five thousand years of Earth cycle should be long enough for any soul to learn. The long cycle is almost over, when there will be great and glorious adjustments on Planet Earth.

There is a very old scripture quote, "For the Lord himself being asked by a certain person when His Kingdom should come," answered, "When two shall be one and that which is without as that which is within." In other words, when the analytical mind becomes one or merged with the higher theta mind, giving us the nine-tenths frozen part thawed out and ready for use. This can be accomplished by more and more communication with your higher or spiritual self.

To get started, here is an example of how simple it is. If the body is in trouble and needs a repair job—just call on the thetan and ask it to patch up the body, make it well and free from sickness. If there is a particular ailment or part of the body that is not well and sound—call on your higher self. It knows how to take care of its own body, having already cared for thousands of bodies. Ask theta very gently and firmly with perfect faith to give you help or the assistance you need. Do this for a few serious minutes several times a day, just to increase and enlarge this precious communication. If you love yourself, it follows you must love the spiritual part. Start talking to your higher self, then be very quiet and wait for the answer that is found only in the higher self or thetan. Keep this up faithfully and you will soon be in good communication, and the two, in time, will be One. Love and communication will start and continue the thaw of the nine-tenths part of the brain.

Why not tap on this great source of power? Instead of so much concern for material things. Pure theta lives and confers eternal joy, never tires or needs any physical thing, but understands all things. To the extent we recognize, contact, and love theta, a big part of its radiance and joy remains in the analytical mind, along with the theta consciousness.

Another comforting fact is there are hundreds of beings on Earth who did not originate here. They had evolved to planets thousands of years more advanced. But out of their love for God and their fellow man, they willingly volunteered to take the Earth cycle, be born on Earth to help build a higher civilization.

This beautiful of all planets is rugged for the souls who came here from other planets, especially so now when the world is more evil than at any other time in its history. Many times these volunteers get stuck deeply in the mud. Being of *Galactic* origin, all the powers of heaven stand by to give all the help and encouragement they can, which is plenty, except they cannot get them out of the Earth mess until the cycle is finished, which will probably be around the year 2000.

The postulate is very strong and is a *superb* tool used by theta. It knows it can make a postulate stronger than steel, yet in the next second, cancel it out and make another one just as strong. We can all use the postulate to our advantage. But, do not expect it to work so quickly. We operate much slower and need more time to decide what we desire. But the biggest difference for us is that our faith is not so sure and positive. The more certainty one has the quicker the postulate works. It is hard for us to know and understand the great power of the postulate. Ron Hubbard uses the word "Certainty" instead of "Faith," which has been worn out in heartbreaking frustration because the absolute power of faith could not be accepted. It seems so fragile and nebulous in a world where evil and material things *seem* so real and powerful. The very opposite is true as it rests on a foundation that God decreed would always have immutable power for those who believe. A quick observation of the world removes all doubt. Material things come and go such as physical bodies, buildings and all things man has created. Can the soul be tested in a laboratory? Seen or felt? Can love be put into a test tube? Faith cannot be heard, seen, or touched. But—there can be no greater power. The material world holds so little power and permanence. But the nebulous quality of spirit is the most positively real element in existence. Man must know the reality of spirit to possess the heaven it brings.

Jesus, the Christ, demonstrated plainly many times how

sure and absolute was the power of faith to work for any one who believes. His infallible words told people they also had the power to do everything He did, and even much greater things; that He of Himself could do nothing; that the Father did the work. But people stuck deeply in the mud could not accept such wondrous truth. Even now, man still does not believe one little word that carries so much power for those who believe and so little for those who do not. God made faith very immutable and strong knowing it had to overcome the heavy material obstacles of man.

The knowingness of the thetan is beyond all understanding. This is much more than the faculty of memory. With Scientology processing the average person can go back while wide awake and alert for thousands of years and instantly answer the questions the Auditor asks concerning present life and past lives.

The conscious mind does not have the data and takes no responsibility for the instant answers. The thetan has complete knowledge of anything it has ever experienced. Time does not exist for the thetan because time is a material man-made consideration. That is why theta recall does not diminish. The thetan lives only in the eternal *now*, with full recall as it is always in the present time.

The auditing is done with what is known as the "E" Meter, which is the most sensitive and accurate instrument for recording all the being has ever experienced from the conscious or theta mind. After using this instrument all over the world for many years, I have never heard of a mistake it has made. It seems to be the greatest source of confirming truth in existence.

To know how faith works we take a good look at the material world, which is the other half. It seems so huge and overpowering, all inclusive, and real, no wonder it swamps the imagination. A big part of the beings on Earth know nothing—or little—about anything except the material with all its negations and evil. We are living in a sea polluted with false and destructive thoughts.

But, we do live on Earth, which is indescribably beautiful, and only God could have created it.

Thetans, like most things are on a gradient scale from evil to good. The ones who choose evil, down grade their power when it is used destructively. The knowingness is lost and they think they have a big deal when they sell their souls to the devil. This is symbolized in drama and opera. The price paid to Satan varies according to the services bought. Sometimes only a part of the soul is sold. In the psychic or unseen —very accurate records are kept, full credit for good is filed along with evil. There are no man made mistakes in record keeping of these files. Satan or negation requires full payment and always collects.

God never created a soul to be eternally lost. No matter how evil, it can work its way back to the source. But the return trip is costly and worth all its costs and much more— because one cannot stand still, we either proceed up or down. The downward path gets worse, finally nothing but suffering and despair until the being finally gets the message or suffers severe insanity. Occultists call this karmic debts which must be paid. This is subject to other considerations because Jesus Christ brought the law of God's forgiveness. Observation indicates the forgiveness of God lifts the burden and confers light. But there is a penalty that must be paid.

I have every reason to know this, because I have spent this life paying the debts of the last life. It is so comforting to know the reason why, and the progressing thetan is so willing to pay all debts. This will be explained more fully in the Chapter on the incarnation of Grassini, the opera singer. The thetan cannot progress very fast when there is any compromise with evil. Unity points out that evil is living in reverse, spelled backward L I V E or E V I L.

There is another thought given to me at this moment. Could this be a part of God's plan to use His law of evolvement and free will to test thetans on the upward path? Remember, life or theta is a supreme gift from God. Thetans all along the time tract are privileged to use this power on any level they chose, with full consequences for their choice. It has been so constituted that it back-fires if used destructively. No being or thing has any power except when given by God.

As constructive theta takes over more and more there are changes. Little things become more important because you are growing in awareness as you experience more of life. Remove the heavy grip of matter, and everything becomes more abundant. Earth, people, everything around you becomes more clear and beautiful. Theta intensifies and re-creates its life force for you as the Oneness grows stronger powerful but indiscernible forces take over so subtly you hardly realize what is happening. During these changes do not be surprised if suddenly for brief periods the old mortal mind of doubt takes over and you are torn to pieces. There is a constant conquest of life over death. Life is stronger—that is why during these negative moments, you should use the powerful antidote of Jesus when he said, "get Thee behind Me Satan." Negation is a fact of life on Earth, but keep it behind you, which destroys its power. Know it is there but the greater power of Theta can subdue it, so that it has no more power over your life. Negation, the dark, unhappy element of Satan fights for its life, too, but wins less and less as theta is strengthened.

Theta pervades everything with its magic. With a deeply loved mate sex becomes more thrilling, unlifting and rejuvenating.

It is the seeming little things that in reality are the big things, because theta brings them in constant flow to put sparkle and umph into living. Besides, if you are in tune with the universe the little things usually grow bigger. Nothing remains the same, growth or regression are the order of life. God's willingness and plans for man are unlimited happiness and progress spiritually.

The only reason we have strife, frustration and sorrow, is to make your belief stronger or as a prod to get us back on the happy path of God's aura of love.

Yes, it is the little things that are the big things. Materialism places wrong values, happiness is a search to discover what are the true values. We look for happiness in the wrong places. These true values can only be found in the observation of life and natural laws. You can only receive happiness in the degree you have given it to others. Selfishness is not the worst fault, but it is the greatest destroyer of happiness.

There can be no greater joy and peace than to know you and the Father are one. This lifts one above trials and considerations of mortal life. In putting aside the mortal conscious mind, one can go straight to the divine and help ourselves to priceless treasures only God can give. Consider the happiness of others first and you will reap rich rewards, which are no longer important. Jesus said, "Seek ye first the Kingdom of God and all else shall be added." After you have found the Kingdom, the realization dawns that the Kingdom of God is all there is.

The short life of Joan of Arc, has always fascinated me. Both her triumphs and tragedy. At the time she lived few people had the gift to communicate through clairaudience. Those who did would not dare let it be known because they could be tagged as witches—which was extremely dangerous. Her background had been a simple and devoutly religious life. She was only sixteen, ignorant and with little experience of the world.

The voices she heard became familiar which she supposed was natural because she lived close to God. The plot thickens quickly when one or more powerful discarnate-thetans wished to play a little game by taking a hand in worldly affairs. I strongly believe God had nothing to do with it. There is no evidence that God controls the actions and free will of His Creations. That would be a violation of his law of evolvement and free will. First these game-loving thetans had to locate a source of communication because an Earth body had to be used and was necessary to their plans. So— pathetic, helpless, little Joan was chosen to supply the body. She probably thought it was God talking to her. It is a fact that anyone having an open channel for Clair Audience, can receive from any living or discarnate source of sending power. The familiar voices told her she had been chosen to lead the French Army to victory.

I leave to your imagination to pick up the thoughts and consternation of the French Army and its high leaders when it was learned an inexperienced, country girl of sixteen years, with no military background was to be in full charge to lead them to victory. Joan's thoughts were no doubt more frightened and confused.

Joan rode in front of the army in complete control. A good bet would be the Army officers rode close by ready to pick up the pieces. As this strange combination took off to win battle after battle with no serious harm to Joan, the Army officers were amazed and stunned, but seeing had to be believing—unless they cherished a secret thought that they were doing the fighting and that Joan was just along for the ride. The army and public could not rate her anything but pure magic.

The King was put back on his throne. The battles all won.

Then, the voices told her to return home, that her work was finished, but she didn't want any part of the dull life back home, not after all the excitement, power and glory. Instead she tried to lead the army again . . . but the power was gone. In desperation she tried to contact the voices again, but there was no power even for that. She believed strongly and wrongly that the power was hers. This is a mistake most people make without thinking. Under the circumstances how could she be blamed? Even though she disobeyed the source of her power, even though it was probably not from God, if she had used her channel to go directly to God, and not just the voices, we wonder if the results would have been different. But she was so young and ignorant, and knew nothing about the psychic power of communication through which she could contact any source capable of receiving. God is all power, but there are many levels of power.

Knowing something about the law of evolvement we can be sure the beings who play rough games, especially with harmless young ones had to pay a heavy price for the fearsome tragedy they caused Joan to suffer. We cannot even close our spiritual eyes to the fact that Joan might have brought great suffering to other beings in past lives. When the final judgment of God comes, only the soul and its lives will be judged. It will be the whole picture or record. But Jesus Christ did bring the law of forgiveness even though there is a remaining penalty. You can be sure Joan paid off a very big debt. Also—where were the game loving thetans or thetan when their girl needed help so desperately?

Deep meditation should be given to this tragic event of history. It has always been disturbing that no power on Earth or heaven came to her rescue. She put the King back on his throne, but he did not lift a finger to help her. The English were afraid of her demonstrated power and are responsible for her death, according to justice which I believe is the highest attribute of God, along with truth. These people, or powers, have no doubt taken heavy responsibility for what happened. This was over a period of only three years. It started at sixteen years of age and ended with her death at nineteen.

We know about humanity all down the ages and man's great inhumanity to man, a large part of history has been the account of the violation of the gift of love, peace and happiness from God. Why does man in general seem to prefer hate, violence and greed? We live on a beautiful planet of abundance, but man corrupts and damages everything he touches. He has contributed so little to his civilization during the last twenty-five thousand year cycle which will soon come to an end. It has been established that about two percent of humanity must drag the ninety-eight percent along the road of progress. It is quite a miracle that God, with only two percent of His Creations, could accomplish so much. The power of good or God is beyond understanding. If twenty-five percent or less could come alive spiritually with great love for God and their fellow man, there would be such a miracle to stagger the imagination, they would come so fast. Man must balance the scales, for God is still in the miracle business. His gifts are loaded heavily on one side. But man must tip the scale with his love and obedience.

The experience of Joan of Arc was included in this book because it is a classic example of the power of spirit or theta —also obedience to God, the Arch Angels, the Hosts of heaven, whose duty it is to guide us, and bring the will of God everywhere.

It is generally believed the end of the age is near. This will be graduation time for the long-age cycle. All who cannot receive a passing grade for the course will be removed to another planet more suitable for their requirements. This planet Earth will be upgraded according to all prophecy.

The remnant who remain are to build a glorious new age of the brotherhood of man. The Bible calls this the millenium. It is also known as the Aquarian age which is ruled by the planet Uranus, whose mission is to clear the decks, so the old, worn out and useless, along with the evil can be destroyed. But not by God. Man is perfectly capable of this, especially now that he has nuclear energy.

8

A Glimpse Into Man's Relation to the Planets

This book would not be complete without a chapter on Astrology. I have always believed in it as a strong influence on all life, but never had the opportunity to study it until 1934. I found my teacher, a brilliant astrologer and occult student. She started her first free classes in January 1912.

Astrologers study deeply for many years. Even then they are mostly born to it, for it requires more than one life time of intense study. This ancient art and science could not be except through reincarnation, because there is a definite thread of continuity through many lives, especially the last past life. The present life is the consequence of the past life and other lives way beyond.

The chart clearly indicates the lessons that have been learned and those that have not. Before I studied astrology, I asked an aunt who was an occult student, if she believed in astrology. Her answer has proved wise and knowing. She said "yes I certainly do, but not in astrologists." The negative here is many students grab a little knowledge and then for a fee, undertake to foretell the future of their clients. The future is only a tendency at best. It is not fated. No wonder there is much confusion, and little accuracy. In spite of this it has survived from before the dawn of civilization and the chaldeans, through the dark ages and still flourishing now in present time.

After all these years, now in 1973 I am still researching to find some missing answers. From a correct birth chart many things are revealed. There can be no doubt of its validity to the serious researcher, yet it does not reveal everything. First it is infinite, and the finite mind of man is limited in understanding the pattern of infinite planning as revealed by the birth chart. The planets are the generators of energy in the Father's kingdom and we in turn pick up this energy and use it wisely or unwisely. The one thing we completely control is our free will choice as to either good or bad. The benefic aspects always make what ever path we choose easier and happier. While adverse aspects create problems, that usually can be handled. Adverse aspects are valuable because if constructively handled they make us strong. If the native is not strong there will not be much achievement or progress any way. We learn to solve our problems from rising above adverse aspects. Unsolved problems grow constantly worse, causing confusion, discord and despair. However all problems are not always ripe for solution and must wait for God to act.

Astrology has been regarded as a fortune telling medium to know about mundane matters, when we get married, have children, money, position. These matters are usually revealed. But serious astrologers hand this out to entice further study and understanding of the main purpose which is to hold the mirror to the soul for a good look and to know more about the higher laws of evolvement.

The entire structure is contained in three parts. Twelve signs of the zodiac. Twelve horoscopal houses and ten planets. All is contained in these three parts. It is the microcosm of the macrocosm. The planets do not compel, only incline. Weak willed natives usually go along with the tide of energy being received. Natives with strong wills get satisfaction of using the gift of free will to build and create whatever they desire.

The conjunction is the strongest aspect, especially if several planets are together, which is a concentration of strength for a special purpose, conferring great power. This power can be used as the native wishes for good or evil. The trine aspect is the most harmonious of all aspects, and is earned by lessons well learned. This is more or less a free gift from heaven, not requiring much effort, just the acceptance. Therefore it is not as strong as the sextile aspect, which gives ability and the opportunity, the native must do the rest, which is a normal condition. The square aspect is adverse, bringing problems which should be solved if the life is to be successful and happy. The opposition lies deeper and requires plenty of soul searching. Through this we are separated from the things we love. But even this can be overcome, through faith, love of our fellow man and God. Then the opposition becomes the conjunction, for there is no evil in the Father's kingdom.

The birth chart clearly indicates generally the personal likes and dislikes, character, talents, personality. But not integrity as that is a matter of free will choice. Astrologers are inclined to think Mercury adverse to Mars inclines the native to be dishonest. I am inclined to the opposite belief. Neither good or bad aspects have anything to do with integrity. A good pickpocket would certainly need Mars and Mercury harmonious to give the necessary dexterity.

The soul coming to birth who has wasted much can not expect to be over blessed with the things it has wasted or hoarded, such as money, sex, food or anything.

Years ago when I looked over the publication, "A Hundred Notable Nativities," I was surprised to find people of great achievement in all lines, wealth, inventions, service and contributions to civilization and progress. All these natives had heavily afflicted charts. I thought about this for a long time when realization came that unless the native was strong enough spiritually to overcome all obstacles and willing to pay any honorable price, he could never be of any value to the society. A very harmonious chart is for the native who is just resting up this time. Thus the adverse aspects are a great challenge to the able and strong.

The influence of the various planets are so well known I will write briefly on all except Neptune, because it is the most mysterious and the least understood, and its influence is necessary and potent at this time.

Jupiter the great benefic of the heavens is the planet through which God expresses in terms of material abundance. A huge and mighty planet, a free giver of everything, never afflicts. Known as the greater benefic of the heavens, it is the extra bonus that gives hope and joy which should keep man on the upward path. Ruler of the ninth house and sign Sagittarius. Each planet generates its own type of energy which merges and works together unified as the complete influence of infinite intelligences upon life and destiny. The qualities of Jupiter are expressed all through nature as abundances, but it is also the planet of conservation and protection. Nothing is wasted or lost, only the form may be changed.

All who would tune in on Jupiter's vibration should be warned to take freely, but nothing should be wasted, destroyed or hoarded. The source of the abundance is always present. Where ever Jupiter is found in the birth chart maps the source of the natives greatest joy.

Jupiter rules the adrenal glands which function to maintain normal emotional balance. In moments of grave danger they act instantly to super charge the reactions, giving unusual strength, quickness of mind, super courage and general acceleration beyond the normal to over come danger and preserve life. Longevity usually comes under Jupiter's influence. As ruler of the ninth house of law which includes all law from man's civil law through to the highest of God's immutable laws that were given before the foundation of the world for the preservation of man and all species.

I bring your attention to the unique qualities of Mercury, the planet of reason, ruler of the third house and the sign Gemini. Here is found the analytical mind, all communications, all travel, transportation, brothers and sisters contracts, agreements, writing and speaking. Mercury has no color or character of its own, it has no emotion except when merged with the influence of another planet. All this as it should be, because it is pure reason. The one little hold out against the great power of emotion. But emotion has no power to compute or think. Mercury is that small voice of reason which must hold the fort against all odds. The sun is always close to Mercury in the chart. As the sun is emotion it is better for Mercury to rise before the sun. Reason should always go before emotion. Mercury must take its color and character from the closest aspect, which is usually the conjunction to the sun, combining reason with emotion.

We all know so well the delightful qualities of Venus, planet of love, beauty, art, harmony and marriage. In the event of marriage be sure to have Venus in the seventh house of marriage at the time the ceremony is performed. Also in a sign harmonious to Venus such as Libra the natural seventh house ruler. Best sign of all would be Pisces, the exaltation sign. Here is combined the tender unselfish compassionate influence of Pisces. Venus is also the negative ruler of Taurus. This because they had to have a ruler for Taurus and Venus seemed the most likely. There is strong belief that the Earth is the positive ruler of Taurus. I go all the way on this. Venus does not have too much affinity for Taurus, but the Earth sure does. Horticulture, love of the

Earth which includes land or real estate. Money also has a strong pull to Earth. Taurians are usually practical down to earth people, who love comfort and money in the bank.

We only have ten positive rulers of the zodiac and we need two more. Earth fits Taurus like the peach skin fits the peach. Mercury does not double very well for the ruler of Virgo. Its ruling planet has not been discovered yet. But occultly it is well known to the Vulcan. The names of the planets are known ages before they are discovered.

The sun, ruler of the sign Leo, the fifth house of the love life and offspring. The sun is powerful and emotional. In the chart it maps the character and individuality. Next to Jupiter the sun is the most benefic of the planets. The giver of life. It is fixed as are its natives. All other planets are pulled around the central magnetism of the sun. Leo rules art and entertainment. The great pull is to the theater where Leo can express through emotion and artistry as the central source to the multitudes. Natives are magnetic, generous, loyal and resourceful. Like all powerful signs if the natives do not respond to the higher concepts of Leo, they tend to sink low into degeneracy.

We could not evolve without the influence of all the planets. But valuable Saturn does not win many awards for popularity, because its mission is to put on the brakes in delays to teach us its lessons of patience, persistence, and caution, which is the very core of achievement. Saturn teaches us to never give up, which builds strength and character. For if we desire something very much, and are willing to pay any honorable price, Saturn will finally say "you win" and hand you your desires. Its gifts are very solid and real, usually money and success. The great ruler of science. Edison is an example. Scientists only win when they never lose hope and faith or give up.

Uranus is the planet of mastery and genius. The action

is sudden and unexpected. Its mission is to tear down the old in order to build the new and progressive. This writer used to think abortion was a cardinal sin, but now thinks just the opposite. No woman should have to give a body to another being, if she does not wish it. No child should be born that is not loved and wanted. I understand that is the way they operate in Japan now. Unless other nations uphold the same concept, Japan will move their civilization way ahead of others. There any woman can have a surgical abortion which is sure fire. No attempted abortion babies will have to go through life handicapped by the basic rejection of not being wanted. Every being born into the world should have the firm foundation of being loved and wanted.

Many new ideas are replacing the old under the influence of Uranus who rules this new age of Aquarius, which began around the turn of the century and will be fairly well established by the year 2000. All the rebellion, strife, crime and unrest we have now are the birth pangs of the new age which will be entirely different according to prophecy and general belief this marks the second coming of Jesus.

Just a few comments on the robust war lord Mars. It is the source of your ability to stand by and fight for anything you desire or for what you believe. It confers energy and red blood and contributes greatly to success when its powers are used constructively. The negative use is senseless fighting and arguments, little or no control over anger, strife in general and war in particular. Mars in harmonious aspect to Venus especially the conjunction gives the strongest love possible between a man and woman. Mars and Venus symbolized by the union of the physical and the spiritual, which is complete love. Jesus Christ did not come into the world to save sinners. That is a convenient misconception. He came to instruct sinners on how to save themselves and to show every being the way to God and eternal joy. Humanity was so dwarfed and evil they whittled God down to their size. They would have us believe that God was cruel, jealous and vindictive, something to be feared. Jesus had to change these wrong concepts before the octave planets could be discovered.

Neptune, the planet of divinity, the tuning fork of the universe, the essence of spirit, Lord of the hidden, undercover twelfth house and the sign Pisces is regarded as a malefic, rightly so for a big majority of people. Neptune and the sign Pisces is symbolized by two fish, one swimming up stream and one down down stream. Very dual in nature as we shall explore.

The positive Neptune carries a very high spiritual vibration. But the negative just the opposite, no half way measures with Neptune. Never violent, always mild, but tricky, strong and dangerous to aberrated or evil beings. The negative Neptune causes insanity, addiction to alcohol and drugs, all forms of fraud. Neptunes mission either benefic or malefic is to give an escape mechanism from the burdens of life. Ruling oil which is an escape from friction. Drugs and insanity an escape from reality, suicide, an escape from life. The difference from the positive and negative is very great, because it is so dual. Hospitals and prisons are under Neptune as ruler of the twelfth house. If one can not accept the positive Neptune, its power is reversed and then only the negative can be contacted. Neptune especially does not work well in a house of human relations such as seventh house of marriage, fourth house of parents, eleventh house of friends, and third house of brothers and sisters. I have never known of a happy marriage for the native who has Neptune in the seventh house.

It is through the Neptune ray that man becomes consciously active upon the limitless, potent, invisible realm of spiritual substance.

The power contained in the physical is like a drop of water in a bucket, compared to the vast power that is contained in spirit. It is on this plane that man contacts his God, where there is only the perfect law of divine love and justice, operating with infallible precision for the highest good. Neptune also confers the understanding faith or certainly when in the midst of apparent ruin or dire need, can cast out all fear and declare that God is an ever present help in any need.

All are more or less familiar with the uplift of consciousness experienced during performances of great drama or music, when the perceptions are stepped up to such an extent that the every day world of heart ache and disappointment, slip into nothingness as a mere transitory illusion of pain and negation, and that now the soul or thetan is released from bondage and is free to stand upon the threshold, to glimpse the true and immortal life of exaltation and beauty God has created and given to all who will accept as their permanent heritage now and forever.

Who is there to testify with the fervor and fire of truth, that the physical plane is all that is real and tangible, while Neptune's mission is to conjur up an illusion to delight and give surcease for the moment?

Also, who can question the omnipotent, merciful Father through His Neptune ray, does permit the weary traveller to open his spiritual eyes when ever he chooses and behold God's true plan for man to those who seek Him, love Him and keep His commandments?

Neptune alone could not reveal the world of spiritual substance. It must merge and work with other planets less nebulous for the full expression.

As the tuning fork of the universe, it is largely responsible for the phenomena of melody, which is an exquisite almost indecernible link between the physical and spiritual realms. Melody is the pure essence of heaven given physical being in

music. A composer works very hard to create music and or-
chestrations that can be played on instruments or sung. But
not so melody. The composers vibratory rate being such that
he may contact and record the vibrations which orginated in
pure spirit. A glorious example of Neptune and Venus
working together.

9

The Octave Planets

The ancients had only seven basic planets from which to make their studies and predictions. As man is ready to receive the energy of the higher or Octave planets, which have always been, but will be discovered only when the time is ripe on the Celestial Calendar to operate in man's destiny and progress.

The last three planets discovered in modern times are known as Octave planets. The energy they create is much like the basic seven, only stepped up an octave in vibration. As in music, the piano keyboard consists of seven basic tones, repeated over and over in octaves—which are the same tones only stepped up to more vibrations per second as it goes higher.

All Nature seems to be in layers or octaves. Actually the only difference between Earth and heaven is the vibratory rate, as this is stepped up more and more, the physical, which is much slower, is left behind.

This being true in music and all life, imagine what man can become as he is stepped up to higher vibrations by the Octave planets. As the vibrations continue to go higher evil will not be able to exist.

Neptune was discovered in 1848 and is the Octave of Mercury, conferring spiritual discernment and communication on all levels.

Uranus discovered a little later is the Octave of Venus. Stepping up personal love to universal love.

Pluto was discovered in 1930 and is the higher Octave of the Moon. Economic in nature; bringing drastic changes especially for women and home conditions; ruler of the sign Scorpio and groups. Cooperation at its best and coersion at its worst. Mars had to play the role as Scorpio ruler because we had to accept even a negative ruler rather than no ruler. Mars being so open and direct was not in tune with Scorpio. Pluto finally came along and is the true positive ruler of Scorpio and the eighth house which includes inherited and insurance money; all under cover manipulations, separations and death.

When a planet is discovered the tendency is to boil off the scum first. The kidnappings, hi-jackings, explosions, organized crime, rebellions and rioting are just a few of the indications that Pluto is boiling off its scum. Before long, Pluto will give us the finished jelly which will be delectable beyond our wildest dreams.

In the world wide conspiracy under way now, by the big rich, including the International bankers, who do not want Communism which is a slave state; they are working for World wide Socialism. This is clearly explained and revealed with pictures and names in a book "None Dare Call It Conspiracy" put out by the John Birch Society. These big powers are not satisfied to possess many billions of dollars. They desire full control over all the World. Of course this will never be because the big issue then would be who is going to be the number one, number two, number three, etc., etc., boss. Also, it is not on the Celestial Calendar of destiny. Time is fast running out on such old fashioned activities. Astrologers note the facts—Scorpio, Pluto and the eighth house tell the story. Pluto, an Octave, is stepping up the Moon to economic grandure. The scum in the making will go down in the garbage can or more correctly to a more suitable planet. Man's cruelty to man will be no more. Love and cooperation will replace that. Women's Lib will seem like a bad dream.

Almighty God created man, male and female in His own image. No after-thought about Adam here, who came eons of time later with his problems in the Garden of Eden, about being lonely and having to play with spare ribs. This Adam was created from dust, not by God from spirit.

Marriages will be made in heaven with both male and female giving a hundred percent, thereby creating another hundred percent by their union of potential power to give back to life and God.

It is fascinating to relax and concentrate on the Octave work by Pluto.

It is a waste of energy and money for each woman to do the marketing, cooking, and wash dishes separately. In the future this will be done on a wholesale basis. There will be large and beautiful eating places with lounges for friends to gather after dinner to visit and exchange thoughts and ideas. Children will be treated as intelligent young adults with no spoiling or down grading.

Under the new economy greater wealth will be created for all, but not the same amounts. Ability and usefulness will always be in command of more. The biggest uplift will be no aberrated people. No prisons, no welfare or mental hospitals. The cutest trick to me will be no more crooked lawyers. They will be useless in the new order.

I do believe there will be a capitalistic system, spiritualized and stepped up to new concepts because God's immutable laws are contrary to any known forms of socialism, which is an unholy control mechanism.

All were not created equal. There is a time difference in evolvement. Bulwer Lytton was a great English writer and occult observer, who wrote in one of his books, quote, "From the time the Earth was thrown off from the Sun as a gaseous mass, inequality is the first law of the universe." This definitely does not rule out equal justice and opportunity. Inequality is proof of the law of evolvement. Even God does not violate His laws. Divine justice gives to all the full right to use these laws for a slower or more rapid evolvement.

People will live much longer, several hundred years, many will never die. Because humans will not live under stress and strain, they will not go into a manic to make millions of dollars, or control others which would be useless and unnecessary. There will be plenty of time for everyone to do their thing, along with contributions to the economy. Love of God and your fellow man will be the key note. When this kind of love is shared by everyone—God will be back in the miracle business in a big way. Who knows? When God receives this kind of love from everyone, even He will go to heights undreamed of now, to give more to His Creations.

10

Romance of Four Planets

When I was a child of eleven years, mythology was my favorite subject, reading everything I could find about it. Among many other stories I read about the Greek God who swam the Hellespont everyday to see the goddess he loved. Then one day while she was waiting on the shore of the sea his dead body was washed up at her feet. End of mythology story.

But me a little girl, had a big grief charge over it, sobbing and crying until the thought came that I had no reason to cry over a remote incident that did not concern me. So by force of reason and will I snapped out of it. But I never forgot.

Many years have passed since the little girl cried. I am living in the country alone, but on a heavily travelled highway. Desolate and lonely because I had recently lost my beloved husband of forty one years.

One day a car drove up but no one came to the door, so I went out to see what the stranger wanted. He told me he was dealing in large acreage tracts which was my husband's greatest interest. He was told I could give him information about the various owners.

Being psychic, I get the truest impressions about people at the first contact. While talking I had the impression he was unhappy and took very little interest in life, but was not willing to throw in the sponge. His mind was in his work, but not his heart. Several times he stopped looking at the landscape, turned around and looked directly at me. Then his face lit up and smiled as if he recognized me, or there was something familiar. He said he would see me again in a few days. But I had no idea I would ever see him again. One week later he drove up with a happy smile and said "I told you I would be back." He has continued to come back ever since. After the third visit it suddenly flashed clear and sure that he was my love who swam the Hellespont. The communications of the Hellespont period and present time were so similar. Being worried aoout the long swim he said there was no need to worry, swimming is the easiest thing he did, that he was an expert or words to that effect. In present time I thought about the long trips on the highways, always driving. He answered "driving is the easiest thing I do and I am careful." This is factual data, but you could hardly expect anyone to connect the two incidents twenty five thousand years apart. But knowing something about the vast powers of the soul with its miracle of recall, it begins to seem possible considering there is only one soul or thetan, that never forgets, never sleeps, or dies and it can be anywhere instantly. The big impact on life is from the thetan. When theta rejects a body, everything is gone, only a mass of decaying chemicals are left behind. So it is not hard to believe that two powerful thetans who loved through the ages would certainly recognize each other upon contact at any time. Just as the identity of my visitor flashed, I cried out to God not to let it happen again.

A month later I had fifty four hours of processing, running a chain on loss of love. The auditor was highly qualified, a fourth level operating thetan. The E-meter was used all during the audit. I was asked how many incarnations with the being we now know as Turnley. The instant answer was seven. Then how many incarnations with the being who swam the Hellespont. Instantly I started to say seven again, but quickly changed it to five, because I had just said seven with Turnley. The auditor looked at the E-meter, which is always hooked up to the pre-clear or patient, and said, "that is not the true answer." I quickly changed the answer to seven and the E-meter was satisfied. That was the only wrong answer in the fifty four hours of auditing. I ran through the high spots of all fourteen incarnations. Most of these incidents erased quickly and are not in the subconscious any longer. But a few remained in my analytical consciousness.

I will recount the Hellespont incident which has not been erased as follows. A happy young woman walked up and down the beach waiting as she did every day to be with the man she loved. She tired as time dragged on and he did not appear, as usual on the horizon. She had been fearful of these long swims. Now fear began to grip her heart, adding to the weariness. The girl became more distressed as she looked for the familiar form swimming toward her. She noticed the dark storm clouds in the distance. She continued to walk up and down the beach thinking he might be off course due to the storm. Finally she did see a body and went into a frenzy of praying to God, "Oh let it be a live body." As it continued to come nearer, hope and prayers turned to heavy grief. As she waded into the water to bring in her lover's lifeless body. She held Tavaras wet body in her arms, putting her kisses all over his face. The flow of heartbreaking tears matched their wet bodies. She thought to love him enough to last for all eternity, and it did.

In present time after I recognized my visitor as Tavara I had the feeling there was a barrier between us, otherwise why did he make the long swim every day? I thought it might have been marriage. But when I ran it later with the auditor and the E-meter I was asked if the barrier was marriage, the instant answer was "no, it was more political in nature." The auditor then asked "were you from different planets?"

The answer was "oh yes, that was the barrier." I did not find my love's name during auditing as it did not come up. But later in present time, I wanted to know the name. It had to come from me as no one else knew. I recovered the name by going into the deep meditation and asking the immortal thetan part of me to give me the name. A little while later I clearly heard the name "Tavara."

Now I will digress a little and write about visitors from outer space, who are greatly more advanced than Earth people. They have been coming to Earth for thousands of years for the sole purpose of helping in our evolvement. Those who came by space craft and were not born here, are more or less limited in the time spent here. Other people of galactic origin who were born here have volunteered to be born here and must take on the full age cycle of about twenty five thousand years.

The temporary visitors not being subject to the negations of Earth, brought much wisdom, love and compassion. That is why it is only natural they were worshipped as Gods, which was not too far wrong, as we are all Gods in the making. When the natives asked where they came from and were told Mount Olympus and as they came in space craft always from above, this gave the concept they were Gods. The goddess Venus got her name by being a native of the planet Venus, which she evidently told them. As usual she came by space and was put down near an ocean beach. So the natives not seeing the quickly vanishing space craft, believed she was created from the foam of the ocean and came to them a full blown beautiful woman. They had a different story about Minerva, goddess of wisdom. The story has it that Zeus, king of the heavens and her father, struck his head a light blow and Minerva sprung from his head fully grown with all her wisdom and intelligence.

The roots of mythology lie deeply in truth, but handed

down through antiquity by races who could not understand the full story. Mythology gradually became the delightful accounts of half truth, born not of lies and deception, but from love and gratitude of people who could never forget through all time.

There is another incarnation with Tavara had with the being now known as Marie Louise. This happened during the glory of the Roman Empire. No exact date on this. They were together again, very much in love and happy, but they only had seven years together, half that time as his mistress and then as his wife.

At this time in history, military affairs were the big thing. Tavara was an officer but was outranked by another higher officer who brought great tragedy to us. I do not know the villain's name then, but I sure do know the name and person to my sorrow in this present incarnation. He chose to become a woman this time. Yes, thetans can change the sex of their bodies in other incarnations if they wish. Possibly he became a woman to get closer to me for a number of aberrated reasons. Also I had to accept her now to pay for what I did to him. I disliked him very much, but he was determined to have the love of Tavara's wife at any cost. So he plotted to order Tavara on a dangerous mission with little chance of his survival. The wife knew it was planned murder but could do nothing to prevent it. Her grief and hatred for the man responsible was intense. The hated man still tried to force his attentions on her. Hate is very negative and should never be indulged in, under any circumstances. The wife also planned carefully by hiding a sharp dagger in the folds of her garment and then pretending to soften a little in order to get close to him so she could put the dagger into his wicked heart, which she sure did, and then drank a deadly poison as she had no desire to live any longer. I paid for what I did as the former me.

Remember Catharine, my step mother in the chapter on significant data? She tried to control my life, breaking up friendships and the love life. As long as I was under her control completely, she was most indulgent and sweet. She did all in her power to keep men from getting near me. After she lost control over me, what passed as love turned to hate. This gives the answer to why I suffered so much through her. No there never was hint or slightest indication of anything homosexual. Note what I brought on myself by killing him. Finally she was taken out of my life as related, but she did get one last wack at me which included Turnley, probably because he was my husband. We had a serious automobile accident that I felt was not normal. We were both in a quiet, happy mood as susal, going to attend a fried chicken dinner where we would be with friends. We had slowed down watching for the left hand turn off the highway, when an oncoming car suddenly skidded and went out of control, backed across the road just ahead of us. No way to stop, Turnley could only jerk the car to the right avoiding a collision directly into the driver's seat. Both cars were demolished. We landed in the hospital, after emergency attention we were put in widely separated rooms. Gentle Turnley put up such a big fight to have us in the same room. The hospital personnel were shocked at such a thing. That had never been allowed. Turnley finally changed their beliefs with the help of the manager.

We had the feeling there was something strange and abnormal about the accident, so we travelled several hundred miles to get Scientology processing. After running out the shock of the impact, we ran a new process called "search and discover." We were asked to name the person in our life who was the most destructive. In one breath we both said "Catharine." So we both wrote her a letter. I knew when she passed on several years before. In our letters we told her we never wished to contact her again, that she had lost all power over us. We wanted her out of our lives forever. We were assured we would never have to worry about her again. We never have and feel quite sure it is forever. We do have more control over our personal affairs than most people think.

There is an apparent loose end in this incident I do not understand. Why did Turnley have to suffer from Catharine when it was another being involved? More processing would probably reveal Turnley too had some involvement. The past records are very accurate if you had them. Strange how many incarnations are lived with so few beings. It would not be high justice according to the law of evolvement if every thing had to be judged after only one life time. Fortunately all these complex situations can be unraveled and disclosed through the power of divine truth and justice. We should be very grateful we are given so many chances to learn.

Another incident on this chain of loss of love, but vastly greater and by far the heaviest of all. This was the walk to Calvary. I followed Jesus along with others of His followers every step of the way. I have said a number of times during good Friday services that I believed I was there but did not remember a thing about it. It was presented on this chain because there was deep love which has always existed.

This walk seemed very long because in running it I felt the heavy pain of exhaustion over the entire body, which was small compared to the agony of mind, heart and soul. No language or arrangement of words could describe it.

All the world knows about this event except for the very last and most glorious gift from Jesus. The auditor used all his skills over and over to run it out. But it would not erase because an event of this magnitude could not be erased. It has been seared into the soul of this immortal thetan. Just at this second as I write I am being told "it will all be erased at my second coming." Oh thank God.

I saw the huddled small groups of His followers in a prone position with heads near the ground, with covers over their bodies and heads. Although it was during the afternoon hours, it was dark. I could not see distinctly. I was not in the body at this time, that is probably why I grasped the truth that Jesus transcended the agony of the body to send out the most powerful miracle of love to remove the deep shock, sorrow and grief from His followers. It is great satisfaction to relate they tried very hard to refuse the gift of peace. His last and greatest gift on Earth. They fought off the strong rays of peace Jesus was sending. Jesus continued to send until those who loved him had to accept His gift of peace and understanding. In the moment of deep concentration it flashes that Jesus also received a large part of the gift which gave ease to His body and mind. Was He entirely forsaken by the Father? And is this gift wishful thinking? I really do not believe it is wishful thinking. The Father never forsakes, but Jesus had to die on the cross not to save sinners. It took his death to reveal His life. His mission was to bring the law of forgiveness and show us the way to God. I firmly believe God did give Him ease of body and mind when it was needed most.

I wonder why His last great act of love has not been known before this. Perhaps it was so sacred and precious it was withheld until now, at a time when the world is so sick and frightened and needs this triumph of love over agony more than at any time. As I write this the tears of emotion flow freely. And I wonder why any one in the world would not adore this great Being of light, joy and love we know as Jesus the Christ.

As Tavara was the name of the being who swam the Hellespont, I will continue to identify him as such and relate the first incarnation. This romance involves two planets. Tavara must have met the being now known as Marie Louise on her native planet. He was attracted so much he sent his space craft to capture and deliver her to his home planet. She was frightened and angry at first, but soon felt a strong attraction for him. They had great happiness together. As this incident is on a chain of loss of love, there probably was loss and separation. But I do not recall running any further data.

The first incarnation with Turnley dates back to seventy thousand years on another planet, highly advanced in technology, but low in civilization. This happened to be run in two parts over a twenty year lapse.

In 1951, a new friend we knew through Dianetics, came to visit us for a few days, bringing with him an old type lie detector instrument. He had never been trained, neither had we, but that did not dampen his enthusiasm in running processes wherever he could find some one to practice on. What he regarded as a new toy, we took very seriously. He started on me first. I was facing the bright sunlight, but had a heavy towel over my eyes which completely blocked the sun. After playing around with some processes, he began to get tired, but I was primed and ready to proceed. About this time I told Clem something strange was happening to me. With the eyes heavily covered I suddenly began to see bright sunlight. Clem gleefully announced, "You are about to run an electronic incident."

Either he was tired or didn't know how to handle such an incident. I knew nothing about this, but was already running the incident full force. I was not in the body. I was behind the body, a little to the right. Me, the being I saw, stood tall and erect, angry, disgusted that I had been lured to destruction. The beautiful gown I was wearing, in soft shades of green and blue, exactly like a French import I had worn in present time for concert work. I was aware of being in a small enclosure and the sun looked like it was filtering through a steel or iron mesh. I could pick up no emotion of personal fear. I knew I had fallen into a theta trap through my own carelessness. At this point, the auditor couldn't handle it and stopped the auditing which was a serious mistake which ended the session abruptly. A trained auditor would have kept me running the incident until all the data could be recovered. This incident was not run again until the audit of April 1971, as follows. I was deeply disturbed because my mate had fallen into what we now call the theta trap. I was promised his safe return if I would meet their terms which was not recalled. In my eagerness to save him, I became careless and we were both destroyed in these deadly electronic force fields that have never been duplicated on Earth. According to L. Ron Hubbard, no power has ever existed that could destroy a soul. But when in these force fields the soul can be down graded and told it has no power, the body is all powerful and strong. This is known as facsimile I, which we on Earth, all share. This is the first big reason for lowered awareness of God and the soul. If my readers know nothing about this, it comes as another shock. But the time has come for the truth to be known why we got into our present condition of little awareness.

When Dr. Hubbard wrote the book on Dianetics, he only planned on removing aberrations from the present life, which it certainly has. Only it did not stop there. Not only are incidents in this life on a chain, but the chain extends back for thousands of years on a chain for many life times. Every thing that has ever happened to the thetan is accurately recorded on a chain, linked together for all time. On running the chain on loss of love, only such incidents are found on this particular chain. Dr. Hubbard opened a Pandora's box with Dianetics. Now he must feel like Atlas holding up the entire world on his shoulders. When he fully realized what he had released, he probably gulped a few times, then rolled up his sleeves and really went to work seriously. Now he has made possible the operating thetan, a reality which for so long was only a vague dream. But even operating thetans are on a gradient scale. Ron Hubbard can not uncover, develop and release from the thetan that which has not always been there. All thetans can be cleared of aberration, but inequality is the first law of the universe. Thetans must evolve according to their own desires and abilities.

Dr. Hubbard should be regarded as one of the great gifts from God, sent to help prepare the way for the glorious new age, and the second coming of Jesus Christ.

The next incident on the loss of love chain was probably on Earth. Turnley ran this incident, not me. He had just finished a week's processing, which usually releases some cognitions. He was taking his usual nap while I was in the kitchen fixing supper. Suddenly he rushed into the kitchen, grabbed the bottle and asked if I would have a drink with him. I answered yes, when you tell me what has disturbed you. He then related while in a light sleep, he heard a neighbor call out, "Sandra," in a weird tone of voice. This keyed in the incident as follows. He saw a girl lying on the ground in the sun wearing skins. It was on the veldt, as he looked he saw a big cat creeping toward her and getting ready to spring. He had a weapon in his hands which he instantly threw at the cat, killing it. But he didn't see the other cat close by that grabbed him at the base of the skull, crushing his head. He had relived that awful moment of shock and pain. No wonder he needed a drink. I said "Now, I will have that drink with you." I have always wondered why I love you so much and am so good to you." I ran the rest of the incident in the 1971 audit. My grief and shock was very heavy, but in time I took another mate.

The next incident was during the Spanish inquisition. I was an entertainer or dancer. They were torturing my love Turnley, to force admissions of heresy. We were not concerned with heresy or such tiresome things. We were only interested in loving and living. They made me listen to his cries of pain, an old worn out trick. Next I was tortured in the same manner, with my love having to hear my cries of pain. Finally some kind of help came or maybe some way, somehow, a little humanity flickered. The recalls on this are dim. It probably has been erased and only a little remains in the analytical mind.

The next incident with Turnley happened only about five hundred years ago. This one was most pathetic and heartbreaking. I was a nun in a convent and Turnley was a priest, always kind, gentle and understanding. With the deep love we had for each other dating back over 65,000 years, the inevitable happened after we got together again. I became pregnant. When the condition could not be kept secret any longer, my love was taken away to some unknown place. I could get no information concerning him, and was kept in some kind of confinement, in a state of grief and shock. What a sad, unhealthy condition for the pathetic little unborn child. After I gave birth, I never saw my child, no information whether it lived or died, or male or female. I could contact nothing but shock, loss and grief. Death was the only possible escape for me. I was kept in a small hospital infirmary. I contacted some concern over me from doctors, nuns and priests, and recall them around my bed which I never left after my child was born. I paid no attention to anything. Everything was blotted from consciousness except the great desire for death. I wanted no part of life, as the soul had lost everything, it simply rejected the body.

Life is strange. After the convent incident, Turnley and I have had two more incarnations. One with Grassini the opera singer, but not as her husband. He was the long suffering, faithful lover and the present incarnation. It has been checked out by the E-meter, that my present time son is the same being as the lost child.

The Catholic Church does the best it can to control people and make them behave according to the best man-made laws. But these are not God's laws. It was not fully realized what enormous raw power is contained in God's laws which they tried to combat.

The going will always be hard and painful when humanity and religion does not snuggle down close to the protection and love of God's immutable laws. Man is aberrated and distorts everything he touches, thinking there must be control in order to achieve well being.

We should be tolerant and understanding of past mistakes, because we need our organized churches with their cohesive power of love to hold civilization together. Based only on God's commandments as revealed by Jesus Christ who takes full responsibility and belongs to planet Earth. Other highly evolved perfected beings take responsibility for their own planets.

11

Life and Loves of Grassini

Grassini was born of humble parents near Milan, Italy on April 8, 1773, and died January 3, 1850, at Milan. This humble birth was not the slightest handicap to her, being highly talented, very beautiful of face, body and voice, and, a great personality. There was not much she lacked except contacts with men in high places. Even this was inevitable. At an early age, about sixteen, she won the friendship of General Belgios. He arranged to have her given the finest instruction that could be found in Milan. She was a hard worker, highly intelligent and made rapid progress, developing a beautiful voice with superb execution and agility to sing the most difficult scores ever written for a singer.

She made her debut in a great opera, "The Virgin of the Sun," in 1794, when she was twenty-one years of age.

Marie Louise signed her first contract to go on tour when twenty years of age.

Grassini soon became the first singer in all Italy, making appearances everywhere and receiving great ovations. She was also a good actress and knew all the arts and tricks of winning audiences.

Marie Louise had to settle for being a star, playing Army Camps and stopping the show at every performance to receive big ovations. Not so much for the beautiful voice but for the art of knowing how to win audiences, especially the all male audiences.

A brief outline of the Grassini career is necessary to relate.

But our interests now are in the personal lives and characters. Marie Louise is not only the reincarnation of Grassini, but also her direct descendant. Great Grandfather Lartigue managed a plantation in the West Indies, which was owned by his family. There was a sudden uprising of the natives and he barely escaped with his life, and the family silver which he hastily wrapped in a napkin. It was dinner time and the table was all set for the meal. He was hidden in an old abandoned well. After dark the friend got him aboard a ship and he landed in South Carolina. He married a South Carolina girl. They had a daughter named Adele Lartigue who was my Grandmother. I had an Aunt and a Sister who had the same name. Strange to relate these three Adele Lartigues died in middle age from strokes. My sister inherited the Lartigue silver.

My grandmother was told my her father that she was the direct descendant of the favorite singer at the Court of Napoleon. There is some confusion about the name. It came down to me as Annie Grace. Perhaps this was an attempt to change the name Grassini to a more English version. One thing is certain, there can be no doubt or confusion about the identity. Records show Napoleon took her to Paris from Italy and gave her a contract to sing at a very high salary at his Court.

Now we go back and take a look at some events that happened before Napoleon became the Emperor of the French. On a certain June first, news reached him his troops had defeated the Austrians who had been in control of Italy. This made everyone happy except the Austrians.

Napoleon thought such an event was worthy of a big triumphal entry into Milan. Being far from Paris at the time, he lacked certain necessary equipment, but he was used to pulling any kind of a rabbit out of nowhere. They found an old dilapidated stage coach which had belonged to the Marchese del Monte. It was hastily repaired, six white horses were found and hitched to the coach. They were happy that everything was in good shape and ready for the trip to Milan. On June 2, they proudly took off for Milan in high spirits to impress the big crowds assembled at Milan waiting to heap full honors and wild cheers on their liberator. But alas, "man proposes but God disposes." Along the road a terrible storm broke loose and they were forced to take shelter. The rain came through the roof of the coach like a sieve. After the rain stopped and they were dried off, they continued their journey, but as fate would have it, another big rain storm started again—this time there was no shelter. The rain came through the roof. The road became deep in mud, the white horses and the entire group became splattered with mud. The high officers following on horseback were a pitiful sight. The beautiful, big waving plumes in their helmets hung down limp and dirty—like old rags. But the lowest thing was their spirits.

At Milan the weather had remained beautiful. All was happy entusiasm. Can you imagine or picture the sight that greeted the happy throng, when that desolate pitiful little group of the great Bonaparte and his high officers, moved slowly into their midst? They would have welcomed the Earth, if it would open up and swallow them. But this did not happen, and there was no place to go but straight into the shocked people of Milan. It was so unexpected and unbelievable they could not hide their shock and disappointment. At this response, Napoleon, who was already deeply humiliated, went into a rage and made no effort to hide it. Being a Leo with Capricorn rising, he was proud and had a volcanic temper.

At this point, the political picture was confused, uncertain and dangerous. A serious crisis could have resulted. People just don't treat the great Napoleon like a stray, mongrel dog.

But quick thinking leaders of Milan went into fast action. Napoleon and officers had gone straight to the ducal palace where they could bathe and change uniforms. A concert was quickly arranged at La Scala Opera House. Flowers, cheers and applause were heaped on him along with shouts of "Long live the liberator of Milan." His Leo pride was somewhat eased but he was not a bit happy.

June the third was a big red letter day. A concert was arranged featuring Grassini, the golden voiced prima donna, whom Napoleon had met several years earlier. At their first meeting he was still in love with Josephine and paid no atten-tion to the singers extraordinarily beautiful face and voice.

Times had changed. This time he showered her with his attention and enthusiasm. This was a big surprise to her. She was quick to remind him, quote, "I made my debut at pre-cisely the same time as the first exploits of the General com-manding the army in Italy. At that time, I was in the first flush of my beauty and my talent, and no one talked of any-thing but me in 'The Virgin of the Sun.' I captured every-one's eyes, I inflamed everyone's heart, you alone remained indifferent, yet it was you alone that I was thinking of. How bizarre and odd, when I heroically disdained it all for a single glance from you. I could not win that glance, now you are showering glances on me at a time when I am no longer worth the trouble, when I am no longer worthy of you." Unquote.

With these remarks, it has been thought she underesti-mated her charms, because she had reached the ripe old age of twenty-seven years. Nothing could be further from the truth. She never underestimated anything about herself. This was her intelligent way of properly conditioning him before she took over. Besides she was still hurt because she could not win the glance she desired so much, and still did.

We skip the big success of the concert on June, the third. The events that followed pushed that into the background.

When Berthier, Bonaparte's personal aide, went to his bedroom the next morning, the Consul was all smiles having breakfast with the prima donna, who was also happy and smiling. She probably had proved she was worth any amount of trouble.

Grassini's art was the most natural and integral part of her being. She carried it with her always, on the stage and off, also into the bedroom. I know what happened during that first night. I was not only there, it was me. I am the only person who has ever known anything about it. I, the immortal being have never separated anything from God. Next to divine justice the highest attribute of God is art.

In Chicago at the entrance to the Fine Arts building is engraved in stone, "All Passes, Art Alone Endures."

The love life, combined with art, becomes superlative. That is why Grassini's love life was an exquisite experience of the spiritual and physical combined. She was exactly the same woman on the stage or in the bedroom, with the same character and talents.

Back to that first night. She gave him a love so gentle and tender, kissing him slowly all over his face and intensely tender on the lips. This was something Napoleon had never known. Josephine was never like this. She probably did the best she could. But she was not Grassini. Then Grassini became gradually more ardent until she gave him her full passion. Then she reached for his soul, and told him about the joy and wondrous love of God, The Supreme Source of everything. Thus God was an integral part of her love life that was natural and as it should be.

Of course she made very serious mistakes which will be fully explained later.

The next morning Napoleon called a meeting of 200 Milanese Priests. This was a shock because he was known to be an Atheist. They heard him say to them, quote, "I wanted all of you gathered together so that I might have the satisfaction of informing you personally of the feelings I have about the Catholic, Apostolic Roman religion. Being convinced that this religion is the only one that can secure true happiness for a well ordered society and strengthen the foundations of good government. I assure you that I will bend all my efforts to protect and defend it at all times and by all means." Unquote.

My goodness, what a terrific shot in the arm, or somewhere, Grassini had given him. Napoleon was so set on strong government that controlled people. In the light of present day events he was quite right. People who cannot control themselves constructively must be controlled for the good of all. Politicians are not statesmen. They care nothing about a well ordered society. Not one drop of altruism is in the big give-away programs with more and more money to people who are not worth anything except their votes that are for sale.

I wish so much we had Napoleon with us now. He would straighten things very quickly. I guess we have not earned him now.

He began to come into power shortly after the dreadful French Revolution. He was horrified at what happened and thought it was senseless and remarked that a few well placed cannon balls would have put a stop to the whole mess quickly.

Now, we have Scientology that is going all out to raise our civilization and prepare a remnant that will build a society that is one with God. But even Scientology, that is so strong in restoring full self determination to people, must control people until they can control themselves.

In this story, it seems we must digress quite often. Now

we go back and finish Napoleon's address to the two hundred Priests.

I think the biographer of Napoleon was a man of little understanding or it might be more kind to say he was not an artist. He added his puny ideas to what Napoleon had to say, quote, "And the man who had just spent the night in the arms of Signorina Grassini, said, quote 'no society can exist without morality, therefore it is the only religion which can provide a strong and enduring support for the state.' " Unquote.

I wonder if the biographer knew Napoleon was an Atheist. If so, why Napoleon's big all out support of the Church, after spending a night in the arms of Grassini? This seems strange unless there is some deeper understanding of her.

A physical voice can be beautiful and well trained, but usually remains just a physical voice. But when the power of spirit is combined with a flawless voice, it is stepped way up in vibration which reaches God, which steps it up still more. When this happens the voice takes on a spiritual loveliness beyond ordinary understanding, gripping the heart and soul of all who hear it. In these moments the singer transcends to full Oneness with God. This is the highest expression of Art and is possessed by very few. These are the great ones, God sends once in a while to give a preview of heaven through glorious music to all who can receive.

Grassini and Marie Louise the immortal being had such power in the voice. These precious genes will never die. Grassini worked hard to build a greater voice for the next body. She will keep on working to build greater voices and always will. Or rather we should say, the One Immortal Being built all the voices. The many bodies had nothing to do with it.

When ready to incarnate as Grassini, it took a good look

at past lives she had lived, loving only one man. Her sorrow was so great at the loss of one love. Remember the Hellespont swim and the Roman Empire incident? Through all these incarnations the Immortal Being was constant and wanted her one love. These things she pondered, so she made a postulate that it would never happen again. Because she would love many men and play the field. Postulates always work, but she could not foresee the great unhappiness for herself and others. During the incarnations of constancy she built up a love so powerful it would never die, once given. Any man who had known her love would never give it up no matter what the consequence. She in turn loved them the same way. It is hard to imagine what unhappiness, heart break and confusion resulted. But God's Commandment was, "Thou Shalt not Commit Adultery."

Any departure from God's laws, made only for our protection and happiness, brings nothing but sorrow and frustration.

When Grassini was ready to incarnate into the body of Marie Louise, she was active again with more postulates. She had no intention of repeating the mistakes of Grassini. She installed sex blocks, only to slow sex down a little, giving more control, with the big emphasis on one love at a time. Grassini would never entirely do away with love, that would ruin the voice. She especially planned on building a much more beautiful voice. So as Marie Louise she chose to be born into a fine, intelligent family, where there were already sex blocks.

Remember the experience at age three? And numbers of others on a chain, in the Chapter "Significant Data"? Grassini, or Marie Louise, came into this world God conscious. The Immortal Being has been severely punished and has suffered greatly for past mistakes. But she is definitely on the upward path of evolvement.

Take a look at my love life, and how much was suffered over these losses and separations. It explains John's extreme jealousy. Turnley was my faithful lover. He suffered so much because I would be gone for several weeks at a time, and he did not know where I was. Even after we were married he held it against me for years. He didn't understand entirely. He would have liked to get as far from me as possible, but he still loved me so much. I wiped the slate clean with him. We were blissfully happy for the last twenty odd years, and had only three crises in the forty-one years together.

Grassini had numbers of lovers besides Napoleon. The list includes Prince Alberico de Belgiojoso, Pierre Rode, a violin-ist Wellington and others. The first one when she was six-teen, Jean Sarvant, in his book says that the Russian Tzar was also one of her lovers.

The block on the sex life had no influence whatsoever on the voice. I was strong, healthy, radiant, enthusiastic, loved everyone, and was so thrilled with the beauty of the voice, and wondered why God had chosen me to receive such a gift. The personality and voice were all Grassini, with only the sex block added. It made me sick all over when a man looked at me with that hated gleam in his eye.

Then one day, I decided to confront the situation. There was a fine, big, good looking man with whom I could be friendly, because he was carrying the torch for another girl. I always wanted and loved children so much—no block there. One day as I looked at him, I had to face the fact that if I ever had a child, I had to accept a man's cooperation, that was the one thing I could not do alone. I had avoided facing this fact for a long time. But—this incident was the begin-ning of overcoming the block. I became the same as Grassini except I only loved one man at a time. I never gave up a man I loved but circumstances or the past mistakes took full charge of these separations. But thank God I never lost a man because I could not hold his love.

Remember Catharine? The most evil influence in my life. She was the villain from the Roman Empire incident, who used his position to bring about the murder of the man I loved. Thetans or spiritual beings do not possess sex having no bodies, but have complete understanding of all things. When reincarnating, they can choose a body of either sex, usually they keep the same sex right on. I have never contacted myself as anything but a woman. I believe I have always been a woman. I enjoy so much having men for the opposite sex.

You will understand much more about Catharine if you will recall the chapter on "Significant Data."

If I had not stuck that dagger into his heart I would not have had to contend with her in this life. Nothing but the body can be destroyed. Kill someone and they take another body and come back—you have them right on your lap. Remember Lily's word, "I would rather God take you from me now than have you grow up to be a bad woman." Remember Catharine's words when she broke up a budding friendship with a very fine man. She said, "I would rather see you dead and in your casket than married to that man." The truth was she would rather see me dead than married to any man. The odds were against her.

Also disturbing were the groups of boys who ganged up on me and followed everywhere they could, from the age of thirteen through fifteen. This is definitely linked to Grassini incarnation. I do not know how this was accomplished. I did not want anything to do with boys, I only wished to repel them. It was some mysterious force at work I could not understand. But it made me feel degraded and unhappy.

Due to the sex block, I did not even know the stork did not bring babies until I was twelve years of age, then Catharine had to tell me. Then asked, "How does the baby get out of the Mother's body?" She said, "Use your own reason, what is the largest opening in the body?" The light quickly dawned and I said, "Oh, she vomits them up." I remained quite dumb until well into fifteen when again Catharine had to tell me the facts. I was horrified and shocked and said that is not the way it should be.

Otherwise, Grassini and Marie Louise were very much alike, being the one and same immortal being.

I knew I had to have at least one child if the genes carry-ing the voice were to be preserved.

When I look at my Grandsons, I have a secret gleeful, impish feeling that they don't realize their value to me. Their Mother being negative like Catharine feels she must control everything. So, she has largely succeeded in keeping me away from them. But the big thing I want she surely cannot con-trol.

There are a few interesting details concerning voice in-struction from one of the greatest teachers in this Country. Adolph Muhlman, who was closely associated with the Dureski brothers, who were grand opera singers in Paris, they devised the greatest method of voice training ever known. They took their art to new heights of perfection. But it had to be mostly psychic, because the voice is not visible. Any good teacher could train a voice by exercises, breath control and placement, but the Dureski brothers went straight to the vocal chords by their psychic methods, which made it difficult to teach or learn.

Once my teacher was trying so hard to give me something very valuable, but intangible. He became so frustrated he lost control and tried to ram his big fist down my throat. I went into a rage, ran away from him, stamped my foot and told him angrily to never let it happen again. I thought deeply about this and knew my teacher was trying very hard to give me something precious and valuable. I decided to go into complete rapport with his mind. Language would not help so much especially as his English was limited. So the latent psychic abilities had to start functioning. One happy day, not long after I completely understood what he could not tell me. He knew instantly by the gorgeous results that I understood perfectly. We both laughed and could not stop laughing. If anyone had opened the studio door they would have thought Muhlman and his pupil had lost their senses, when in truth, we had just found some valuable senses.

I traveled for several years with Italian singers doing grand opera presentations. I was happy with them. We lived almost as one family. But it was not the opera career I longed for.

Finally, an emotional conflict developed. I wanted opera with my heart and soul, but I also wanted a husband and offspring even more.

Gina, the manager, was one of the most delightful and lovable people I had ever known. She used to tell me she could not love me any more if I were her own child. I think I was her child of the Grassini incarnation. Gina's family had always lived in Milan for generations which was the place of Grassini's birth and death.

Gina's step father was the greatest opera conductor Italy had ever produced. He always memoried every detail of the complex opera score. As Gina had a beautiful dramatic so-prano voice it was easy for her to become a star singer. All was fine until the little demon of fate took a hand. A hand-some young understudy had to sing the leading role with Gina and they became madly in love with each other. At that time, she was engaged to a prominent doctor. She be-came pregnant, which brought complications. So, as she tells it, they escaped and came to New York where they were married at once at City Hall. The child someway did not survive. That is why their careers had to be in the United

States, where I contacted her. Coincidence? No such thing. All is divine order.

The last time I saw Gina, she had plans made for me to have a big operatic career. The planned details would take several years to work out through her many prominent contacts in Italy and other sure considerations. She told me again she loved me like her own child.

The conflict had been going on for sometime, and I made the painful choice because I wanted love and offspring more than anything else. There are no regrets, the present life is exactly as it should be.

Although the immortal being knows everything that has happened to it, but in between bodies and experiences, nature has a way of gently putting a light veil over the consciousness so as not to complicate or over burden the current life with material too heavy to handle.

But with processing or greater understanding, this light veil is lifted by the thetan, then the analytical part is free to know all with happiness.

This brings to mind an experience I had after three weeks of processing. This happened while the body was asleep. It seems after great effort, I had my soul or thetan backed up against a stone wall and I was looking straight at my higher self. I said with gusto, "Now I have you right where I want you. There is nothing the soul does not know. I want to know everything you know, now start talking." The higher self answered, "Just how happy would you be if you knew everything? The thetan installs forgetfulness and confusions to lighten the burden of the current life." I answered, "I want to know, it would not affect my happiness or well being. If it happened to me, I want to know about it."

My readers all know I did find out so much from the distant past. It has been a great relief and satisfaction. I feel like a heavy load has been lifted. I take the lessons from these past experiences, and put the residue in the garbage can. It is said that full recall is full sanity.

In the delightful book, "The Sky People" by Brinsley Le Poer Trench, published by Neville Spearman, 112 Whitfield Street, London:

"Reproduction is different on the higher planets. There must be a male and female and they must perform in such a manner to consciously produce offspring. But not the same bodily contact of Earth people."

From the book, "The Mystical Life of Jesus Christ" offered by the Rosacrucian Fellowship, A.M.O.R.C., of Oceanside, California, we find related the missing part in the life of Jesus from age thirteen to thirty.

Joseph and Mary, along with Saint Anne, who was the mother of Mary and the wife of the high priest, belonged to the Essene order, a non Hebrew religious group.

When age thirteen the Essene order took full charge of the training and education of Jesus, who was known to be the holy child. But no chances could be taken. He had to be proven to be the long promised Messiah.

Jesus was taken to one great sacred but hidden mystery school after another, until he was ready to start his ministry at age thirty. His training was most thorough and extensive. He never made an error, or failed in the tiniest point. Always perfect, glorious and with love supreme. He proved He was the only begotten son of God, using a physical Earth body.

At the finish of His training there was the greatest initiation ever known on planet Earth, somewhere in the depths of the Pyramids. The details were so sacred, it could never be released to ordinary mortals.

This explains how the virgin birth was accomplished with the male factor supplied by the Angel Gabriel.

Remember the three miraculous births of the Bible? Gabriel visited these three women before the births. Sarah, wife of Abraham, Elizabeth, and Mary.

From so much unknowingness—I have offered a terrific shot of knowingness—to think about for a long time, or, forget quickly. It all depends on how much your mind and soul yearns to know the truth that will set you free to trod the glorious paths to eternity.

Truth is exciting and alive.

Eternal and supreme.